Affiliate Marketing Mastery

Harness the Power of Affiliate Marketing to Build a Lucrative Online Business in the Digital Age

Lewis Finan

Table of Contents

Introduction

In the vast landscape of the digital age, where opportunities unfold at the speed of a click and innovation shapes the way we do business, one strategy has emerged as a powerhouse for entrepreneurs seeking to carve their path to success—Affiliate Marketing. Welcome to "Affiliate Marketing Mastery: Harness the Power of Affiliate Marketing to Build a Lucrative Online Business in the Digital Age."

The digital revolution has not only transformed the way we connect, communicate, and consume information but has also ushered in a new era of entrepreneurship. In this era, traditional business models have given way to dynamic, online ventures that thrive on adaptability and creativity. At the forefront of this paradigm shift is Affiliate Marketing—a concept that has evolved into a cornerstone for many successful online businesses.

This book is your comprehensive guide to understanding, implementing, and mastering the art of affiliate marketing. Whether you're a seasoned entrepreneur looking to diversify your income streams or a newcomer eager to explore the vast landscape of online business, the principles and strategies within these pages will be your roadmap to success.

Why Affiliate Marketing?

Affiliate Marketing offers a unique opportunity for individuals to leverage the power of established brands and products without the complexities of creating and maintaining them. By becoming an affiliate, you enter into a symbiotic relationship with product creators and vendors. As you drive traffic and generate sales, you earn a commission—a win-win scenario where success is shared.

In "Affiliate Marketing Mastery," we will delve into the core principles of affiliate marketing, exploring how to choose the right products, build a robust online presence, and implement effective marketing strategies. From understanding the psychology of consumer behavior to optimizing your digital assets for maximum impact, each chapter is crafted to equip you with the knowledge and skills needed to thrive in the competitive world of affiliate marketing.

What to Expect

This book is more than just a manual; it's a journey that takes you from the basics to advanced strategies, providing actionable insights, real-world examples, and case studies that illuminate the path to success. Whether you're looking to create a sustainable passive income stream or scale your online business to new heights, "Affiliate Marketing Mastery" is your trusted companion.

Let's embark on this transformative journey together, as we unravel the secrets, strategies, and nuances of affiliate marketing. Get ready to harness the power of affiliate marketing and build a lucrative online business in the digital age. The future of your success awaits.

Understanding the Digital Age

The Digital Age, a term synonymous with the rapid evolution of technology, has transformed every facet of our lives, reshaping the way we connect, communicate, and conduct business. It is an era where the boundaries between the physical and digital worlds blur, giving rise to unprecedented opportunities and challenges. To navigate this ever-changing landscape, it's crucial to grasp the fundamental shifts that define the Digital Age.

The Rise of Connectivity

At the heart of the Digital Age is connectivity. The advent of the internet, social media, and mobile devices has woven a seamless web that connects people, businesses, and ideas across the globe. In this interconnected world, information flows at an unprecedented pace, breaking down geographical barriers and fostering a sense of global community.

The Power of Information

Never before has information been so accessible. The Digital Age has democratized knowledge, placing vast amounts of information at our fingertips. Search engines and online platforms have become gateways to a wealth of data, empowering individuals to learn, explore, and make informed decisions like never before. However, with this accessibility comes the challenge of navigating through the vast sea of information and discerning the credible from the misleading.

E-Commerce Revolution

Commerce has undergone a paradigm shift in the Digital Age. E-commerce platforms have redefined the way we shop, allowing consumers to browse, compare, and purchase products with a few clicks.

Businesses, both large and small, now have a global storefront, reaching customers beyond traditional boundaries. The rise of online marketplaces and digital payment systems has revolutionized the buying and selling experience, making transactions faster, more efficient, and increasingly secure.

The Digital Workspace

The traditional office is no longer confined to brick-and-mortar walls. The Digital Age has given rise to remote work, collaborative platforms, and virtual communication tools, transforming the way we work. With the flexibility of working from anywhere, businesses can tap into a global talent pool, fostering diversity and innovation.

Data: The New Currency

In the Digital Age, data is a valuable currency. Every online interaction generates a trail of data that businesses analyze to understand consumer behavior, tailor services, and drive strategic decisions. While this data-driven approach offers unprecedented insights, it also raises concerns about privacy, security, and ethical use.

Constant Innovation

The Digital Age is characterized by relentless innovation. Breakthroughs in artificial intelligence, blockchain, augmented reality, and other technologies continue to reshape industries and create new possibilities.

Staying relevant in this era requires a mindset of continuous learning and adaptability.

Understanding the Digital Age is not just about navigating technology; it's about embracing a mindset of agility, curiosity, and ethical responsibility. As we stand at the intersection of the physical and digital realms, the choices we make today will shape the trajectory of this transformative era. The Digital Age is a canvas of endless possibilities, awaiting the strokes of innovation, connectivity, and human ingenuity.

The Evolution of Online Business

The landscape of commerce has undergone a profound transformation with the evolution of online business. From its humble beginnings as a novel experiment to its current status as a global economic powerhouse, the journey of online business reflects not just a shift in medium but a fundamental change in how we perceive, initiate, and sustain commercial activities.

1. The Dawn of E-Commerce:

The story begins with the birth of e-commerce, an era marked by the emergence of websites and online marketplaces. The late 20th century saw the first online transactions, pioneering a shift from traditional brick-and-mortar stores to virtual storefronts. The convenience of shopping from the comfort of one's home laid the groundwork for a digital retail revolution.

2. The Rise of Internet Giants:

As the Internet gained prominence, a few visionary companies seized the opportunity to establish themselves as internet giants. Amazon, eBay, and later, Alibaba, redefined the retail landscape, offering an extensive array of products and services with unparalleled convenience. These platforms not only disrupted traditional retail but set the stage for a new era of online entrepreneurship.

3. The Birth of Digital Marketing:

With the rise of e-commerce, digital marketing emerged as a crucial element in the success of online businesses. Search engine optimization (SEO), social media marketing, and online advertising became essential tools for reaching and engaging a global audience. Businesses learned to harness the power of data analytics to refine their strategies and connect with their target markets more effectively.

4. The Era of Content and Community:

As the internet matured, content became king. Online businesses began focusing on building engaging content to attract and retain customers. Content marketing, influencer collaborations, and community building became integral components of online business strategies. Brands realized the importance of not just selling products but also creating a meaningful connection with their audience.

5. Mobile Revolution and App Economy:

The widespread adoption of smartphones propelled online businesses to new heights. Mobile apps became a primary interface for consumers, enabling seamless shopping experiences, personalized recommendations, and instant transactions. The app economy gave rise to a new wave of entrepreneurs, disrupting industries through innovative mobile solutions.

6. The Advent of Ecosystems:

In recent years, online businesses have evolved beyond standalone platforms. Ecosystems have emerged, where businesses integrate seamlessly with various services to provide a holistic experience. From e-commerce platforms offering payment services to social media platforms facilitating direct sales, interconnected ecosystems have become a hallmark of the modern online business landscape.

7. The Influence of Artificial Intelligence:

Artificial intelligence (AI) has become a game-changer in online business. From chatbots enhancing customer support to personalized recommendations based on machine learning algorithms, AI has elevated the level of personalization and efficiency in online interactions. It continues to shape the way businesses operate and cater to individual customer needs.

8. Sustainability and Ethical Business Practices:

As online businesses have proliferated, there's a growing emphasis on sustainability and ethical practices. Consumers are increasingly conscious of the environmental and social impact of their purchases. Online businesses are responding by adopting eco-friendly practices, promoting transparency, and aligning with ethical values to build trust and loyalty.

The evolution of online business is a dynamic journey, marked by technological advancements, changing consumer behaviors, and the relentless pursuit of innovation. As we navigate this ever-shifting landscape, one thing remains clear: the world of online business will continue to evolve, presenting new opportunities and challenges for entrepreneurs ready to adapt and innovate.

Chapter 1: Fundamentals of Affiliate Marketing

In the vast realm of online entrepreneurship, Affiliate Marketing stands out as a dynamic and lucrative strategy for individuals looking to generate income by promoting products and services. This chapter delves into the fundamentals of Affiliate Marketing, providing a solid foundation for understanding its principles, mechanisms, and potential for financial success.

1. What is Affiliate Marketing?

Affiliate Marketing is a performance-based marketing strategy where individuals, known as affiliates, earn a commission for promoting and driving sales or leads to products or services. It operates on a symbiotic relationship between affiliates, merchants (product creators or vendors), and consumers. Affiliates act as intermediaries, leveraging their marketing efforts to connect consumers with products they might be interested in.

2. How Affiliate Marketing Works:

The core of Affiliate Marketing lies in the affiliate's ability to earn a commission for each sale or action generated through their unique affiliate link. This link serves as a tracking mechanism, attributing sales or leads back to the affiliate. When a consumer clicks on the affiliate link and makes a purchase or completes a desired action, the affiliate earns a predetermined commission.

3. Key Players in Affiliate Marketing:

Affiliates: These are individuals or entities that promote products or services and earn commissions for driving desired actions. Affiliates can range from individual bloggers to large media companies.

Merchants (Vendors): Merchants are the businesses or individuals who create and own the products or services. They leverage affiliates to expand their reach and increase sales.

Consumers: Consumers play a vital role in the Affiliate Marketing ecosystem. Their actions, such as making a purchase or signing up for a service, trigger the affiliate commission.

4. Types of Affiliate Marketing:

Pay-Per-Sale (PPS): Affiliates earn a commission when the referred customer makes a purchase.

Pay-Per-Lead (PPL): Affiliates earn a commission when the referred customer takes a specific action, such as filling out a form or signing up for a trial.

Pay-Per-Click (PPC): Affiliates earn a commission based on the number of clicks generated through their affiliate link, regardless of whether a sale is made.

5. Choosing Profitable Niches and Products:

Success in Affiliate Marketing often hinges on choosing the right niche and products. Affiliates should conduct thorough research to identify profitable niches with a demand for the products or services they intend to promote. Assessing competition, understanding the target audience, and evaluating product quality are crucial steps in making informed choices.

6. Building Trust and Credibility:

Building a successful affiliate marketing venture requires establishing trust with your audience. Affiliates who authentically share their experiences, provide valuable content, and recommend products based on genuine belief are more likely to cultivate trust and credibility. This trust, once earned, can significantly impact the effectiveness of affiliate marketing efforts.

As we journey deeper into the world of Affiliate Marketing, this chapter lays the groundwork for understanding the essential concepts that form the backbone of a successful affiliate business. From the dynamics of the affiliate ecosystem to the strategies for selecting profitable niches, mastering the fundamentals is key to unlocking the full potential of Affiliate Marketing in the digital age.

1.1 What is Affiliate Marketing?

Affiliate Marketing is a performance-based marketing strategy in which individuals, known as affiliates, earn a commission by promoting products or services offered by other businesses or individuals. This marketing model operates on a symbiotic relationship between affiliates, merchants (product creators or vendors), and consumers.

Here's a breakdown of how Affiliate Marketing works:

1. **Affiliates**: These are individuals or entities who sign up for affiliate programs and promote products or services using unique affiliate links. Affiliates can employ various channels such as websites, blogs, social media, or email marketing to reach potential customers.
2. **Merchants (Vendors)**: Merchants are the businesses or individuals who own the products or services. They create affiliate programs to leverage the marketing efforts of affiliates. Merchants benefit by expanding their reach and increasing sales without incurring upfront marketing costs.
3. **Consumers**: Consumers play a pivotal role in the Affiliate Marketing process. When a consumer clicks on an affiliate's unique tracking link and makes a purchase or completes a desired action (such as signing up for a service), the affiliate earns a commission. The consumer, in turn, gains access to a product or service that they may not have discovered otherwise.

The key mechanism of Affiliate Marketing involves the use of unique affiliate links. These links are assigned to each affiliate and serve as a tracking tool. When a consumer clicks on an affiliate's link and makes a purchase, the system attributes that sale to the specific affiliate, ensuring they receive the appropriate commission.

There are various compensation models in Affiliate Marketing:

- **Pay-Per-Sale (PPS)**: Affiliates earn a commission when the referred customer makes a purchase.

- **Pay-Per-Lead (PPL)**: Affiliates earn a commission when the referred customer takes a specific action, such as filling out a form or signing up for a trial.
- **Pay-Per-Click (PPC)**: Affiliates earn a commission based on the number of clicks generated through their affiliate link, regardless of whether a sale is made.

Affiliate Marketing is a dynamic and scalable way for individuals to monetize their online presence and for businesses to increase their sales without extensive upfront advertising costs. Success in Affiliate Marketing often involves strategic product selection, targeted marketing efforts, and the cultivation of trust with the audience to drive conversions and build long-term partnerships.

1.2 How Affiliate Marketing Works

In the intricate tapestry of online commerce, Affiliate Marketing emerges as a dynamic and mutually beneficial strategy, connecting businesses with a vast network of marketers. Understanding the mechanics of Affiliate Marketing requires unraveling the intricacies of its processes, the key players involved, and the strategies that fuel its success.

1. **The Foundations:**

At its core, Affiliate Marketing is a performance-based model where individuals, known as affiliates, earn a commission for promoting products or services and driving desired actions, such as sales or leads.

This model thrives on collaboration, forming a three-way partnership among affiliates, merchants (product vendors), and consumers.

2.   Key Players in the Affiliate Marketing Ecosystem:

Affiliates: These are the driving force behind Affiliate Marketing. Affiliates can be individuals, bloggers, influencers, or even businesses that sign up for affiliate programs. Their role is to promote products or services using unique affiliate links and drive potential customers to the merchant's site.

Merchants (Vendors): Merchants are the businesses or individuals who own the products or services. They create affiliate programs, define commission structures, and provide affiliates with promotional materials. Merchants benefit by expanding their market reach through the efforts of affiliates without incurring upfront marketing costs.

Consumers: The end-users, or consumers, play a crucial role in the Affiliate Marketing cycle. When they click on an affiliate's unique tracking link and complete a desired action, such as making a purchase, the affiliate earns a commission. Consumers gain access to products or services they may not have discovered without the affiliate's promotion.

3.   The Affiliate Link and Tracking Mechanism:

The linchpin of Affiliate Marketing is the affiliate link. Each affiliate is assigned a unique tracking link that helps monitor and attribute sales or leads generated through their promotional efforts. This link, when clicked by a consumer, not only directs them to the merchant's site but also serves as a tracking mechanism to credit the affiliate for the referral.

4. Compensation Models:

Affiliate Marketing offers flexibility in compensation models, allowing businesses to choose the structure that aligns with their goals. The primary models include:

- Pay-Per-Sale (PPS): Affiliates earn a commission when the referred customer makes a purchase. This model aligns incentives, as affiliates are rewarded for driving actual sales.
- Pay-Per-Lead (PPL): Affiliates earn a commission when the referred customer takes a specific action, such as filling out a form or signing up for a trial. This model is common in industries where direct sales may have a more extended cycle.
- Pay-Per-Click (PPC): Affiliates earn a commission based on the number of clicks generated through their affiliate link, irrespective of whether a sale is made. This model emphasizes driving traffic to the merchant's site.

5. Choosing Profitable Niches and Products:

Strategic product selection is crucial for affiliate success. Affiliates often conduct extensive research to identify profitable niches and products with demand in the market. Factors such as competition analysis, understanding the target audience, and evaluating the quality of products contribute to informed decision-making.

6. Building Trust and Credibility:

Successful affiliates go beyond mere promotion; they build trust and credibility with their audience. Authenticity, transparency, and providing valuable content contribute to cultivating a relationship of trust. Affiliates who genuinely believe in the products they promote are more likely to establish long-term connections with their audience.

7. The Affiliate Marketing Journey:

Signing Up for Affiliate Programs: Affiliates begin by joining affiliate programs relevant to their niche. This involves submitting an application, which is often reviewed by the merchant to ensure alignment with their brand values.

Receiving Affiliate Links: Upon approval, affiliates receive unique tracking links. These links are embedded in their promotional content, ensuring that any traffic or sales generated through those links are credited to them.

Creating Content: Affiliates employ various channels to promote products, such as blogs, social media, YouTube, or email marketing. The content created may include reviews, tutorials, or promotional materials designed to resonate with the target audience.

Driving Traffic: The primary goal is to drive targeted traffic to the merchant's site. This involves leveraging SEO strategies, social media engagement, and other marketing techniques to increase visibility and attract potential customers.

Earning Commissions: When a consumer clicks on the affiliate link and completes the desired action, such as making a purchase, the affiliate earns a commission. Commissions vary based on the agreed-upon terms set by the merchant.

8. Tools and Resources for Affiliate Success:

Affiliates often utilize a range of tools and resources to optimize their efforts:

Analytics and Tracking Software: Tools like Google Analytics or affiliate network dashboards provide insights into the performance of affiliate campaigns.

SEO Strategies: Affiliates may employ search engine optimization techniques to enhance the visibility of their content and drive organic traffic.

Email Marketing: Building and nurturing an email list allows affiliates to maintain a direct line of communication with their audience, promoting products and providing valuable content.

Social Media Platforms: Leveraging social media channels helps affiliates reach a broader audience and engage with potential customers.

9. The Evolution of Affiliate Marketing:

Affiliate Marketing has evolved alongside the broader landscape of online commerce. Innovations such as influencer marketing, video content, and the integration of artificial intelligence continue to shape the way affiliates promote products and engage with their audience.

10. Challenges and Opportunities:

While Affiliate Marketing presents numerous opportunities, it is not without its challenges. Increased competition, changes in search engine algorithms, and the need to adapt to evolving consumer behaviors require affiliates to stay agile and continuously refine their strategies.

In conclusion, Affiliate Marketing is a dynamic and scalable model that has empowered individuals and businesses to monetize online influence. From understanding the fundamentals to navigating the evolving landscape, successful affiliates leverage strategic thinking, authenticity, and technological tools to create a sustainable and lucrative online business. As the digital realm continues to evolve, so too will the strategies and possibilities within the realm of Affiliate Marketing.

Chapter 2: Building a Solid Foundation

In the dynamic realm of Affiliate Marketing, success hinges on the establishment of a robust foundation. This chapter explores the essential elements that contribute to building a solid groundwork for a flourishing affiliate business. From cultivating the right mindset to mastering key skills, we delve into the foundational aspects that set the stage for sustainable success in the competitive landscape of online marketing.

1. Developing the Affiliate Mindset:

Building a solid foundation begins with cultivating the right mindset. Successful affiliates approach their work with dedication, resilience, and a continuous learning attitude. Understanding the long-term nature of affiliate marketing and embracing the iterative process of improvement are crucial components of the affiliate mindset. This chapter explores the mindset shifts necessary for navigating the challenges and seizing the opportunities inherent in the world of affiliate marketing.

2. Setting Clear Goals:

Clarity of purpose is fundamental to success in affiliate marketing. Affiliates must set clear, measurable, and achievable goals that align with their overall business objectives. Whether the goal is to generate a certain level of income, build a loyal audience, or expand into new niches, having a well-defined roadmap provides direction and motivation. This section guides affiliates in crafting meaningful and realistic goals to drive their efforts.

3. Understanding Your Audience:

At the heart of successful affiliate marketing lies a deep understanding of the target audience. Affiliates must invest time in researching and defining their audience's needs, preferences, and pain points. By creating detailed buyer personas, affiliates can tailor their content and promotional strategies to resonate with their audience, fostering a connection that goes beyond mere transactions. This chapter explores effective audience research techniques and strategies for building a community around your affiliate brand.

4. Selecting Profitable Niches:

The choice of niche plays a pivotal role in the success of an affiliate business. This section guides affiliates through the process of niche selection, emphasizing the importance of balancing passion and profitability. Affiliates will explore methods for evaluating the demand, competition, and monetization potential within a niche. Strategic niche selection ensures that affiliates invest their time and efforts in areas with the greatest likelihood of success.

5. Building an Online Presence:

A solid foundation requires a strong online presence. Affiliates must establish a professional and user-friendly platform, whether it's a website, blog, or social media profile. This section provides practical insights into creating compelling content, optimizing for search engines, and fostering engagement with the audience. Building a brand that resonates with the target audience is paramount for long-term success in affiliate marketing.

6. Creating Quality Content:

Content is the cornerstone of any successful affiliate marketing strategy. Affiliates must produce high-quality, valuable content that not only attracts visitors but also builds trust and credibility. This chapter explores content creation techniques, including writing compelling product reviews, crafting engaging blog posts, and producing multimedia content such as videos and podcasts. Affiliates will learn how to strike a balance between promotional content and providing genuine value to their audience.

7. Leveraging Social Media:

In the interconnected world of digital marketing, social media is a powerful tool for affiliates to amplify their reach. This section delves into strategies for leveraging platforms such as Instagram, Facebook, Twitter, and LinkedIn to connect with a broader audience. From crafting impactful social media campaigns to utilizing paid advertising effectively, affiliates will gain insights into maximizing their presence across various social channels.

8. Building an Email List:

Email marketing remains a cornerstone of successful affiliate strategies. Building and nurturing an email list allows affiliates to maintain direct communication with their audience, promote products, and deliver valuable content. This chapter explores the process of creating lead magnets, optimizing opt-in forms, and developing effective email campaigns. Affiliates will discover how an engaged email list can become a powerful asset for driving conversions and building long-term relationships.

9. Embracing Analytics and Data:

Data-driven decision-making is essential in the world of affiliate marketing. Affiliates must embrace analytics tools to gain insights into the performance of their campaigns, understand user behavior, and identify areas for improvement. This section provides guidance on setting up analytics tools, interpreting key metrics, and refining strategies based on data-driven insights. Affiliates will learn how to optimize their efforts for maximum impact and return on investment.

Building a solid foundation in affiliate marketing requires a holistic approach that encompasses mindset, goal-setting, audience understanding, niche selection, online presence, content creation, social media leverage, email marketing, and data-driven decision-making. This chapter serves as a comprehensive guide, equipping affiliates with the knowledge and skills needed to establish a resilient and thriving affiliate business in the competitive digital landscape.

2.1 Niche Selection Strategies

Selecting the right niche is a critical determinant of success in affiliate marketing. Niche selection involves finding a specific market segment with both demand and profitability. Here are effective strategies to guide affiliates in choosing a niche that aligns with their goals and maximizes their potential for success:

1. **Passion and Knowledge:**

Choosing a niche based on personal passion and expertise can be a powerful strategy. When affiliates are genuinely interested in and knowledgeable about a subject, their enthusiasm often translates into authentic and compelling content. This passion not only sustains motivation but also resonates with the audience, building credibility and trust.

2. **Research and Analysis:**

Conduct thorough research to identify niches that align with market trends and consumer demands. Tools like Google Trends, keyword research tools, and industry reports can provide valuable insights. Analyze competition to gauge the level of saturation and identify opportunities for differentiation. A balance between demand and manageable competition is key.

3. Evergreen Niches vs. Trending Niches:

Consider the longevity of a niche. Evergreen niches, such as health and wellness, personal finance, or self-improvement, maintain consistent demand over time. On the other hand, trending niches may offer short-term opportunities but could fade in popularity. Striking a balance between evergreen stability and trending potential can be a strategic approach.

4. Monetization Potential:

Evaluate the monetization potential of a niche. While passion is essential, affiliates must ensure there are viable products or services to promote within the chosen niche. Explore affiliate programs, products, and services available in the market to ascertain the revenue potential and commission structures.

5. Audience Identification:

Understanding the target audience is crucial. Affiliates should choose a niche where they can relate to and connect with the audience. Identify the problems, needs, and preferences of the target demographic. Tailoring content to address these aspects enhances the affiliate's ability to resonate with their audience.

6. Sub-Niche Specialization:

Consider narrowing down to sub-niches for specialized targeting. Instead of a broad category, affiliates can focus on specific segments within a niche. For example, within the fitness niche, specialization could be in-home workouts, yoga for beginners, or high-intensity interval training (HIIT). Specialization allows affiliates to become authorities in a specific area.

7. Affiliate Program Evaluation:

Research and evaluate available affiliate programs within potential niches. Analyze commission rates, cookie durations, and the reputation of affiliate programs. Choose niches where reputable affiliate programs offer fair compensation for the effort invested.

8. Trend Monitoring:

Keep an eye on industry trends and emerging markets. Staying informed about technological advancements, cultural shifts, or new consumer behaviors can uncover opportunities for affiliates. Early adoption of trends can position affiliates as industry leaders.

9. Test and Iterate:

Once a niche is selected, it's important to continuously test and iterate. Monitor the performance of content, track affiliate links, and analyze data. If a particular niche or strategy isn't yielding the desired results, be open to adjusting the approach or exploring new niches.

10. Diversification:

Consider diversifying across multiple niches to spread risk and explore various revenue streams. Diversification allows affiliates to adapt to changes in consumer preferences and market dynamics. However, it's essential to maintain a balance to avoid spreading resources too thin.

In conclusion, niche selection is a strategic process that involves a combination of personal interest, market research, audience understanding, and an evaluation of monetization potential. By employing these niche selection strategies, affiliates can position themselves for success in the competitive landscape of affiliate marketing.

2.2 Identifying Profitable Products

Identifying profitable products is a pivotal step in the success of an affiliate marketing venture. It requires a strategic approach that combines market research, understanding consumer needs, and evaluating the potential for monetization. Here are key strategies to help affiliates identify products with the highest likelihood of profitability:

1.   Market Research:

Conduct thorough market research to identify products that are in demand. Utilize tools like Google Trends, keyword research tools, and industry reports to gauge the popularity and search volume of specific products. Analyzing trends and consumer behavior provides valuable insights into the market landscape.

2. Affiliate Program Exploration:

Research and explore reputable affiliate programs within your niche. Look for programs that offer competitive commission rates, reliable tracking systems, and fair payment structures. Choose programs from trusted affiliate networks or directly from product vendors to ensure transparency and reliability.

3. Product Relevance to Your Audience:

Select products that align with the interests, needs, and preferences of your target audience. Understanding your audience allows you to choose products that resonate with them, increasing the likelihood of successful promotions and conversions.

4. High-Quality and Credible Products:

Promote products that are of high quality and have a positive reputation. Consumer trust is paramount in affiliate marketing, and endorsing credible products builds trust with your audience. Consider the reputation of the product vendor and the reviews of the products you plan to promote.

5. Monetization Potential:

Evaluate the monetization potential of products by considering factors such as the product's price point, the average order value, and the commission rate offered by the affiliate program. Choosing products with higher price points and reasonable commission rates can enhance your earnings per sale.

6. Evergreen Products vs. Trending Products:

Consider the longevity of the products you choose to promote. Evergreen products, which maintain consistent demand over time, provide stable earning opportunities. However, there may also be opportunities to capitalize on trending products for short-term gains. A balanced approach that includes a mix of both can be effective.

7. Product Lifecycle:

Understand where a product is in its lifecycle—whether it's a new release, a well-established product, or one experiencing a resurgence. Different stages of a product's lifecycle present unique opportunities and challenges for affiliates. New products may have less competition, while established products may have a proven track record.

8. Seasonal and Holiday Considerations:

Take advantage of seasonal trends and holidays when selecting products. Certain products experience increased demand during specific seasons or holidays. Tailor your promotional efforts to align with these trends and capitalize on the heightened interest in relevant products.

9. Competitive Analysis:

Analyze the competitive landscape within your niche. Identify competing affiliates and assess the strategies they employ. Understanding what products other affiliates are promoting, and how, can help you identify gaps or areas where you can differentiate yourself.

10. Product Accessibility and Affiliate Tools:

Choose products that are easily accessible to your audience. Consider factors such as shipping options, product availability, and geographic targeting. Additionally, assess the availability of affiliate tools and promotional materials provided by the affiliate program, as these resources can facilitate your marketing efforts.

11. Testing and Optimization:

Engage in testing and optimization to refine your product selection strategy. Monitor the performance of different products, track conversion rates, and analyze data to identify which products are yielding the best results. Continuously optimize your approach based on the insights gained through testing.

By implementing these strategies, affiliates can identify profitable products that align with their audience, leverage market trends, and maximize their earning potential in the dynamic landscape of affiliate marketing.

Chapter 3: Creating Compelling Content

In the intricate world of affiliate marketing, content serves as the linchpin that connects affiliates with their audience. The ability to produce compelling, valuable, and engaging content is not just an art but a strategic imperative. This chapter explores the essential elements of creating content that captivates, resonates, and drives conversions in the dynamic landscape of affiliate marketing.

1.   The Power of Compelling Content:

Compelling content is the driving force behind successful affiliate marketing campaigns. It goes beyond mere promotion, aiming to educate, entertain, and inspire the audience. This section delves into the transformative impact of compelling content on building trust, establishing authority, and fostering long-term relationships with your audience.

2.   Understanding Your Audience:

Creating content that resonates begins with a deep understanding of your audience. Explore their preferences, pain points, and interests. By developing detailed buyer personas, affiliates can tailor their content to address the specific needs of their audience. This section provides actionable insights into audience research techniques to inform content creation.

3.   Crafting Engaging Product Reviews:

Product reviews are a cornerstone of affiliate marketing. Crafting engaging and authentic product reviews is an art that involves striking a balance between promotions and providing valuable insights. Affiliates will explore techniques for writing comprehensive and trustworthy reviews that guide consumers in making informed purchasing decisions.

4.   Developing Compelling Blog Posts:

Blogging remains a powerful medium for affiliates to share in-depth insights, trends, and product recommendations. This section explores the elements of creating compelling blog posts, from attention-grabbing headlines to structuring content for readability. Affiliates will learn how to leverage storytelling and visual elements to enhance the impact of their blog content.

5.   Exploring Multimedia Content:

The digital landscape thrives on diversity, and multimedia content offers affiliates an opportunity to connect with their audience through various channels. From creating engaging videos for platforms like YouTube to launching podcasts that provide valuable information, this section delves into the world of multimedia content creation and its role in enhancing audience engagement.

6. Leveraging Social Media Content:

Social media platforms are dynamic spaces that demand tailored content strategies. Affiliates will explore techniques for creating impactful content on platforms such as Instagram, Facebook, Twitter, and LinkedIn. From crafting compelling captions to designing visually appealing graphics, this section provides insights into leveraging social media content for maximum reach and engagement.

7. Building an Email Content Strategy:

Email marketing remains a direct and effective channel for affiliate communication. Crafting an effective email content strategy involves more than just promotional messages. Affiliates will learn how to create engaging newsletters, deliver valuable content to their subscribers, and optimize email campaigns to drive conversions.

8. SEO Strategies for Content Optimization:

Visibility in search engine results is paramount for the success of affiliate content. This section explores Search Engine Optimization (SEO) strategies to enhance the discoverability of affiliate content. From keyword research to on-page optimization, affiliates will gain insights into optimizing their content for search engines and attracting organic traffic.

9. Balancing Promotional and Value-Driven Content:

A successful affiliate content strategy strikes a delicate balance between promotional and value-driven content. This section provides guidance on weaving promotional messages seamlessly into content while maintaining the integrity of valuable information. Affiliates will learn how to foster trust by prioritizing the needs and interests of their audience.

10. Adapting to Emerging Content Trends:

The digital landscape is ever-evolving, and staying ahead requires an awareness of emerging content trends. From the rise of interactive content to the impact of voice search, this section explores trends that are shaping the future of content creation in affiliate marketing. Affiliates will gain insights into adapting their strategies to remain at the forefront of industry trends.

11. Content Distribution Strategies:

Creating compelling content is only half the battle; effective distribution is equally crucial. This section explores strategies for distributing content across various channels, from social media platforms to email newsletters. Affiliates will learn how to amplify their reach and ensure their content resonates with the widest possible audience.

In conclusion, creating compelling content is an art and a science that requires a deep understanding of the audience, strategic optimization for search engines, and adaptation to emerging trends. This chapter serves as a comprehensive guide, equipping affiliates with the knowledge and skills needed to craft content that not only captivates but also drives the success of their affiliate marketing endeavors.

3.1 Content Marketing Essentials

In the ever-evolving landscape of digital marketing, content stands as the cornerstone of successful engagement, brand building, and audience connection. Content marketing, when executed strategically, not only captures attention but also fosters relationships, establishes authority, and drives desired actions. This section explores the essentials of content marketing, providing a roadmap for creating and deploying content that resonates with your audience.

1. **Understanding Content Marketing:**

At its core, content marketing is the creation and distribution of valuable, relevant, and consistent content to attract and retain a defined audience. Unlike traditional advertising, content marketing aims to provide information and insights that align with the audience's interests, needs, and pain points. This approach builds trust and credibility, positioning the brand or individual as a valuable resource.

2. **Identifying Your Target Audience:**

The foundation of effective content marketing lies in a deep understanding of your target audience. Identify your audience's demographics, preferences, and behaviors. Develop detailed buyer personas to guide your content strategy. The more accurately you can tailor your content to your audience's needs, the more impactful and relevant it becomes.

3.   Establishing Clear Objectives:

Define clear and measurable objectives for your content marketing efforts. Whether the goal is to increase brand awareness, drive website traffic, generate leads, or boost sales, having well-defined objectives provides direction and allows for meaningful performance measurement.

4.   Creating High-Quality Content:

Quality is paramount in content marketing. Create content that is informative, engaging, and adds value to your audience's lives. This includes blog posts, articles, videos, infographics, and other formats that align with your brand voice and resonate with your audience. High-quality content builds trust and keeps your audience coming back for more.

5.   Consistency is Key:

Consistency in content creation and distribution is essential for building a loyal audience. Establish a regular publishing schedule that aligns with your audience's expectations. Consistency not only reinforces your brand presence but also contributes to search engine visibility and audience retention.

6.   Search Engine Optimization (SEO):

Optimizing your content for search engines is crucial for improving discoverability. Conduct keyword research to understand the terms your audience uses. Incorporate relevant keywords naturally into your content, titles, and meta descriptions. SEO-friendly content enhances your visibility on search engine results pages.

7.   Utilizing Various Content Formats:

Diversify your content formats to cater to different audience preferences. This includes blog posts, podcasts, videos, infographics, and interactive content. Experimenting with diverse formats allows you to reach a broader audience and keeps your content strategy dynamic.

8.   Storytelling for Engagement:

Storytelling is a powerful tool for creating emotional connections with your audience. Craft narratives that resonate with your brand values and the aspirations of your audience. A compelling story enhances engagement, makes your content memorable, and strengthens the bond between your brand and consumers.

9.   Building a Content Calendar:

Organize your content creation and distribution efforts through a well-structured content calendar. Plan ahead, align content with marketing campaigns and events, and ensure a balanced mix of topics. A content calendar streamlines your workflow, maintains consistency, and helps you adapt to industry trends.

10. Audience Interaction and Engagement:

Encourage audience interaction by responding to comments, questions, and feedback. Foster a sense of community around your content. Engaging with your audience not only strengthens relationships but also provides valuable insights into their preferences and needs.

11. Analyzing Performance Metrics:

Regularly analyze key performance metrics to assess the effectiveness of your content marketing strategy. Metrics such as website traffic, engagement rates, conversion rates, and social media analytics provide valuable insights. Use these insights to refine your approach, identify successful strategies, and address areas for improvement.

12. Adapting to Industry Trends:

Stay abreast of industry trends and emerging technologies. Content marketing is dynamic, and adapting to changes ensures your strategies remain effective. Embrace new platforms, technologies, and content formats to stay relevant and maintain a competitive edge.

In essence, content marketing is a multifaceted discipline that requires a holistic approach. By understanding your audience, setting clear objectives, creating high-quality content consistently, and adapting to industry trends, you can build a content marketing strategy that not only attracts but also engages and retains a loyal audience, driving sustained success for your brand or business.

3.2 SEO Strategies for Affiliate Marketers

Search Engine Optimization (SEO) is a crucial component of success for affiliate marketers. A well-optimized online presence increases visibility, attracts organic traffic, and enhances the overall effectiveness of affiliate marketing efforts. Here are essential SEO strategies tailored for affiliate marketers:

1. **Keyword Research:**

Conduct comprehensive keyword research to identify terms and phrases relevant to your niche and products. Utilize keyword research tools to understand search volume, competition, and user intent. Incorporate these keywords naturally into your content, including product reviews, blog posts, and other promotional materials.

2. **Quality Content Creation:**

Develop high-quality and informative content that adds value to your audience. Search engines prioritize content that is relevant, comprehensive, and user-friendly. Focus on solving problems, answering questions, and addressing the needs of your audience. Well-crafted content not only improves SEO but also enhances user experience.

3. On-Page Optimization:

Optimize on-page elements such as title tags, meta descriptions, headers, and image alt text. Ensure that each page has a clear and concise title reflecting the content. Craft compelling meta descriptions that encourage clicks. Use headers to structure content logically, and include relevant keywords where appropriate.

4. Product Reviews and Descriptions:

For affiliate marketers, product reviews play a pivotal role. Optimize product review content by incorporating target keywords naturally. Provide detailed information about the products, their features, benefits, and potential drawbacks. User-generated content, including reviews and testimonials, can also contribute to SEO.

5. Internal Linking:

Implement a strategic internal linking strategy to connect related content across your website. Internal links help search engines understand the structure of your site and establish a hierarchy. They also guide users to relevant information, improving overall user experience.

6. Backlink Building:

Acquire high-quality backlinks from reputable websites within your niche. Backlinks are a crucial ranking factor, signaling to search engines that your content is valuable and trustworthy. Seek opportunities for guest posting, collaborate with influencers, and leverage industry relationships to build a diverse and authoritative backlink profile.

7. Mobile Optimization:

With the increasing prevalence of mobile device usage, ensuring your website is mobile-friendly is essential for SEO. Google prioritizes mobile-responsive sites in search results. Optimize your site for various devices, enhance page load speed, and provide a seamless user experience on smartphones and tablets.

8. Page Load Speed:

Page load speed is a critical factor in both user experience and search engine rankings. Compress images, leverage browser caching, and utilize content delivery networks (CDNs) to optimize page load times. A faster website improves user satisfaction and contributes to higher search rankings.

9. Schema Markup:

Incorporate schema markup to provide additional context to search engines about the content on your site. Schema markup can enhance the appearance of your snippets in search results, making them more informative and engaging for users.

10. Regular Content Updates:

Frequently update and refresh your content to signal to search engines that your website is active and relevant. This could involve adding new information, updating product reviews, or publishing fresh blog posts. Regular updates show a commitment to providing current and valuable information to your audience.

11. Monitoring Analytics:

Regularly monitor SEO analytics using tools like Google Analytics. Track key metrics such as organic traffic, click-through rates, and conversion rates. Analyzing this data provides insights into the effectiveness of your SEO strategies and allows for continuous improvement.

12. Adaptation to Algorithm Changes:

Stay informed about changes in search engine algorithms and adjust your SEO strategies accordingly. Search engines regularly update their algorithms, and staying ahead of these changes ensures that your website maintains its visibility and rankings.

By incorporating these SEO strategies into your affiliate marketing efforts, you can optimize your online presence, increase organic traffic, and enhance the overall effectiveness of your affiliate business in the competitive digital landscape.

Chapter 4: Establishing Your Online Presence

In the digital realm, the establishment of a robust online presence is the bedrock of success for affiliate marketers. This chapter explores the fundamental steps and strategies involved in creating a compelling and influential online presence. From building a user-friendly website to leveraging social media platforms, each element contributes to a cohesive online identity that resonates with your audience and maximizes the impact of your affiliate marketing efforts.

1.   Crafting Your Online Brand:

Building a powerful online presence begins with defining your brand. Articulate your values, mission, and unique selling propositions. Develop a cohesive brand identity that encompasses visual elements, messaging, and the overall tone. A well-defined brand provides a foundation for creating a consistent and memorable online presence.

2.   Website Development and Optimization:

Your website serves as the digital headquarters of your affiliate marketing efforts. Invest in a user-friendly and visually appealing website that aligns with your brand. Optimize the website for search engines (SEO) by incorporating relevant keywords, improving page load speed, and ensuring mobile responsiveness. A well-optimized website enhances both user experience and search engine visibility.

3.   Domain Selection and Hosting:

Choose a domain name that reflects your brand and is easy to remember. Select a reliable hosting provider to ensure optimal website performance and minimal downtime. The right domain and hosting lay the groundwork for a stable and professional online presence.

4.   Content Creation and Blogging:

Create valuable and engaging content to showcase your expertise and attract your target audience. Blogging is a powerful tool for consistently delivering content to your audience. Develop a content calendar, covering topics relevant to your niche, and establish yourself as a go-to resource in your field. Regular content creation contributes to SEO, audience engagement, and thought leadership.

5.   Social Media Engagement:

Leverage social media platforms to extend your reach and engage with your audience. Choose platforms that align with your target demographic and the nature of your content. Consistent and authentic engagement on platforms such as Instagram, Twitter, Facebook, and LinkedIn enhances your brand visibility and fosters a community around your affiliate marketing endeavors.

6. Email Marketing Strategy:

Build and nurture an email list to maintain direct communication with your audience. Develop a robust email marketing strategy that includes newsletters, promotional offers, and valuable content. Email marketing allows you to deepen relationships with your audience, promote affiliate products, and drive conversions.

7. Multimedia Content Creation:

Diversify your content by incorporating multimedia elements. Create engaging videos, podcasts, and visual content that resonate with your audience. Platforms like YouTube and podcast directories offer additional channels for reaching and connecting with your audience. Multimedia content enhances user experience and caters to varied audience preferences.

8. Search Engine Optimization (SEO):

Prioritize SEO to improve your website's visibility on search engines. Conduct keyword research, optimize on-page elements, and build high-quality backlinks. A well-optimized website increases organic traffic, ensuring that your content is discovered by individuals actively searching for information in your niche.

9. Interactive Elements:

Incorporate interactive elements into your online presence to enhance user engagement. Polls, quizzes, and surveys encourage audience participation, providing valuable insights and fostering a sense of community. Interactive elements contribute to a dynamic and engaging online environment.

10. Community Building:

Cultivate a community around your brand and affiliate marketing efforts. Encourage discussions, respond to comments, and create a sense of belonging for your audience. A thriving community enhances brand loyalty and can serve as a powerful advocacy tool for your affiliate products.

11. Analyzing Metrics and Iterating:

Regularly analyze key metrics to evaluate the performance of your online presence. Monitor website analytics, social media engagement, and email campaign metrics. Use these insights to iterate and optimize your strategies continuously. A data-driven approach ensures that your online presence evolves in line with audience preferences and industry trends.

12. Staying Adaptable to Trends:

The digital landscape is dynamic, with trends and technologies evolving rapidly. Stay adaptable by monitoring industry trends, emerging platforms, and technological advancements. Embrace new opportunities and adjust your online presence to align with the changing preferences of your audience.

Establishing a compelling online presence is an ongoing process that requires a combination of strategic planning, consistent content creation, and adaptability to industry dynamics. This chapter serves as a guide, equipping affiliate marketers with the knowledge and strategies needed to build and maintain a robust online presence that resonates with their audience and drives the success of their affiliate marketing endeavors.

4.1 Building a Website or Blog

In the digital landscape, a well-crafted website or blog serves as the central hub for your online presence, acting as the primary platform for showcasing your content, engaging your audience, and promoting affiliate products. This guide outlines the essential steps to help you build a professional and effective website or blog that aligns with your brand and goals.

1. Define Your Purpose and Goals:

Clearly define the purpose of your website or blog and set specific goals. Whether it's to share expertise, promote affiliate products, or establish an online presence, having a clear vision will guide the design and content creation process.

2.   Choose a Domain Name:

Select a domain name that reflects your brand, is easy to remember, and relates to your niche. Use a reputable domain registrar to secure your chosen domain. Ideally, the domain should be short, memorable, and relevant to the content you plan to share.

3.   Select a Reliable Hosting Provider:

Choose a reliable hosting provider to ensure your website is consistently accessible to visitors. Consider factors like server speed, uptime guarantees, and customer support. Popular hosting providers include Bluehost, SiteGround, and HostGator.

4.   Install a Content Management System (CMS):

Opt for a user-friendly Content Management System (CMS) to build and manage your website. WordPress is a widely-used and beginner-friendly option, offering a vast array of themes and plugins to customize your site. Other CMS options include Joomla and Drupal.

5. Choose a Responsive Theme:

Select a responsive and mobile-friendly theme for your website. A responsive design ensures your site adapts seamlessly to various devices, providing an optimal viewing experience for visitors on desktops, tablets, and smartphones.

6. Customize Your Design:

Personalize the design to align with your brand. Customize colors, fonts, and layout elements to create a cohesive and visually appealing website. Ensure that the design complements the nature of your content and enhances user experience.

7. Create Essential Pages:

Build essential pages such as Home, About Us, Contact, and a Privacy Policy page. These pages provide essential information about your brand, establish credibility, and facilitate communication with your audience.

8. Implement SEO Best Practices:

Optimize your website for search engines by incorporating SEO best practices. This includes using relevant keywords in your content, optimizing Meta tags, and creating a logical site structure. SEO-friendly websites are more likely to rank higher in search engine results.

9. Generate High-Quality Content:

Create compelling and valuable content that resonates with your target audience. Regularly update your blog with informative articles, product reviews, and engaging multimedia content. High-quality content not only attracts visitors but also encourages them to return.

10. Integrate Affiliate Links Strategically:

Integrate affiliate links seamlessly into your content. Ensure that the placement of affiliate links feels natural and relevant to the context. Disclose your affiliate relationships transparently to build trust with your audience.

11. Incorporate Multimedia Elements:

Enhance your content with multimedia elements such as images, videos, and infographics. Visual elements not only make your content more engaging but also cater to different learning preferences among your audience.

12. Implement Call-to-Action (CTA) Buttons:

Guide your visitors toward desired actions by incorporating clear and strategically placed call-to-action buttons. Whether it's encouraging them to subscribe to your newsletter or explore affiliate products, well-designed CTAs enhance user engagement.

13. Ensure Website Security:

Implement security measures to protect your website and its visitors. Keep your CMS, plugins, and themes updated to patch vulnerabilities. Use SSL encryption to secure data transmission, and regularly backup your website to prevent data loss.

14. Enable Social Media Integration:

Facilitate social media sharing by integrating social media buttons into your website. This encourages visitors to share your content across various platforms, expanding your reach and increasing brand visibility.

15. Test and Optimize:

Regularly test your website's functionality and performance. Check for broken links, optimize loading times, and ensure a seamless user experience. Use analytics tools to track visitor behavior and make data-driven optimizations to improve your site's effectiveness.

Building a website or blog is an iterative process that requires ongoing attention and optimization. By following these steps and staying attuned to the needs of your audience, you can create a compelling online platform that not only showcases your content but also effectively supports your affiliate marketing endeavors.

4.2 Leveraging Social Media Platforms

In the dynamic landscape of digital marketing, social media platforms play a pivotal role in expanding your reach, engaging with your audience, and promoting affiliate products. This guide outlines effective strategies to leverage various social media platforms, enhancing your online presence and driving success in your affiliate marketing endeavors.

1. Choose the Right Platforms:

Identify social media platforms that align with your target audience and content type. For visual content, Instagram and Pinterest might be suitable, while Twitter and LinkedIn may be more effective for text-based or professional content. Focus on platforms where your audience is most active.

2. Optimize Your Profiles:

Create professional and engaging profiles on each selected platform. Use a consistent profile picture, a concise and compelling bio, and a link to your website or affiliate products. A well-optimized profile establishes credibility and encourages users to explore your content.

3. Develop a Content Strategy:

Plan a content strategy that resonates with your audience and aligns with the nature of each platform. Create a mix of content types, including product reviews, educational content, visuals, and interactive posts. Tailor your content to suit the preferences of each platform's user base.

4.   Consistent Branding:

Maintain consistent branding across all social media platforms. Use the same logo, color palette, and tone of voice. Consistent branding helps users recognize your content and strengthens your overall online identity.

5.   Engage with Your Audience:

Actively engage with your audience by responding to comments, asking questions, and participating in discussions. Foster a sense of community by acknowledging your followers and creating a dialogue. Engagement boosts the visibility of your content and enhances the overall user experience.

6.   Utilize Visual Content:

Visual content is highly engaging on social media. Use high-quality images, infographics, and videos to capture attention. Platforms like Instagram, Pinterest, and TikTok are particularly visual-centric and offer opportunities for creative expression.

7. Incorporate Hashtags Strategically:

Research and use relevant hashtags to increase the discoverability of your content. Hashtags categorize your posts, making them searchable and allowing you to tap into trending topics. However, use hashtags judiciously to avoid overcrowding your captions.

8. Collaborate with Influencers:

Explore collaboration opportunities with influencers in your niche. Influencers can introduce your affiliate products to their followers, expanding your reach and building credibility. Choose influencers whose audience aligns with your target demographic.

9. Run Contests and Giveaways:

Boost engagement and attract new followers by running contests and giveaways. Encourage participants to share your content or tag friends for a chance to win. Contests not only create excitement but also contribute to the virality of your posts.

10. Schedule Posts Strategically:

Schedule your posts at times when your audience is most active. Use social media scheduling tools to plan and automate your content distribution. Consistent posting, whether daily or weekly, helps maintain audience interest.

11. Share User-Generated Content:

Encourage your audience to create and share content related to your affiliate products. User-generated content adds authenticity to your brand and showcases real-world usage. Share and celebrate user-generated content to strengthen community bonds.

12. Monitor Analytics:

Regularly monitor analytics on each platform to assess the performance of your content. Track metrics such as engagement rates, click-through rates, and follower growth. Use these insights to refine your content strategy and focus on what resonates with your audience.

13. Paid Advertising:

Consider using paid advertising on social media platforms to amplify your reach. Platforms like Facebook, Instagram, and LinkedIn offer targeted advertising options to reach specific demographics. Paid advertising can complement your organic efforts and enhance visibility.

14. Stay Informed About Algorithm Changes:

Social media algorithms evolve, impacting the visibility of your content. Stay informed about algorithm changes on each platform and adjust your strategy accordingly. Adapting to algorithm updates ensures that your content remains prominently featured.

15. Cross-Promote Across Platforms:

Cross-promote your content across different social media platforms. Share snippets, teasers, or unique content on each platform, encouraging users to follow you on other channels. Cross-promotion maximizes your visibility and diversifies your audience.

By implementing these strategies, you can effectively leverage social media platforms to enhance your online presence, engage with your audience, and drive the success of your affiliate marketing initiatives. Social media serves as a dynamic and influential channel for connecting with your audience in the digital age.

Chapter 5: Finding and Joining Affiliate Programs

In the expansive realm of affiliate marketing, the foundation of success lies in strategic collaborations with affiliate programs that align with your niche and audience. This chapter delves into the essential steps and considerations for finding and joining affiliate programs, providing a roadmap for affiliates to forge lucrative partnerships and maximize their earning potential.

1.   Understanding Affiliate Programs:

Before embarking on the journey of finding and joining affiliate programs, it's crucial to grasp the fundamental concept of affiliate marketing. Affiliate programs are arrangements where affiliates promote products or services for merchants and earn a commission for every sale or action generated through their unique affiliate links.

2.   Identifying Your Niche and Audience:

Define your niche and target audience to guide your affiliate program selection. Understanding your niche helps you identify relevant products or services that resonate with your audience, increasing the likelihood of successful promotions.

3. Researching Affiliate Programs:

Conduct thorough research to identify reputable and suitable affiliate programs within your niche. Explore affiliate networks, individual merchants, and industry-specific programs. Consider factors such as commission rates, cookie durations, and the quality of the products or services offered.

4. Affiliate Network Exploration:

Affiliate networks serve as intermediaries connecting affiliates with a multitude of merchants. Explore reputable affiliate networks such as ShareASale, CJ Affiliate, and Rakuten Advertising. These networks simplify the process of finding and joining multiple programs within a centralized platform.

5. Merchant and Product Evaluation:

Evaluate the credibility and reputation of merchants before joining their affiliate programs. Consider the quality of their products or services, customer reviews, and the merchant's overall track record. Choosing reputable merchants enhances your credibility as an affiliate.

6. Commission Structures and Payment Terms:

Examine the commission structures offered by affiliate programs. Some programs offer fixed commissions, while others provide tiered structures or performance-based incentives. Additionally, review payment terms, including payout thresholds and frequency, to ensure they align with your financial goals.

7. Cookie Duration:

Cookie duration refers to the timeframe during which affiliates earn commissions for a user's actions after clicking their affiliate link. Longer cookie durations provide affiliates with extended earning opportunities. Evaluate and choose programs with cookie durations that complement your marketing strategies.

8. Affiliate Program Policies:

Thoroughly review the terms and policies of affiliate programs. Pay attention to restrictions, promotional guidelines, and any exclusivity clauses. Adhering to program policies ensures a harmonious and compliant affiliate partnership.

9. Application Process:

Initiate the application process for selected affiliate programs. Provide accurate and detailed information about your promotional methods, audience demographics, and online presence. Some programs may have specific criteria for approval, so tailor your application accordingly.

10. Affiliate Program Approval:

Upon submitting your application, await approval from the affiliate program. Merchant approval processes vary, with some programs offering instant approval and others requiring manual review. Be prepared to comply with any additional requests or requirements from the program.

11. Accessing Affiliate Resources:

Upon approval, access the affiliate dashboard and familiarize yourself with available resources. Most affiliate programs provide promotional materials, tracking tools, and reporting features. Utilize these resources to optimize your promotional efforts and track your performance.

12. Diversifying Your Affiliate Portfolio:

Consider diversifying your affiliate portfolio by joining multiple programs. This diversification provides a safety net against changes in individual programs and allows you to explore a variety of products or services within your niche.

13. Performance Tracking and Optimization:

Implement robust tracking mechanisms to monitor the performance of your affiliate marketing efforts. Track clicks, conversions, and commissions using affiliate tracking tools and analytics. Analyze the data to optimize your strategies and focus on high-performing programs.

14. Staying Informed About Program Changes:

Affiliate programs may undergo changes in commission structures, policies, or product offerings. Stay informed about program updates by regularly checking communication channels, newsletters, or announcements from the affiliate programs you are a part of.

15. Building Long-Term Relationships:

Cultivate long-term relationships with affiliate programs and merchants. Communicate effectively, adhere to program guidelines, and stay proactive in optimizing your promotional strategies. Building strong relationships contributes to ongoing success in the affiliate marketing landscape.

By navigating the process of finding and joining affiliate programs with a strategic approach, affiliates can establish a diverse and lucrative portfolio, align with reputable merchants, and pave the way for sustained success in the dynamic realm of affiliate marketing.

5.1 Researching and Selecting Affiliate Programs

In the dynamic world of affiliate marketing, the process of researching and selecting affiliate programs is a pivotal step that directly influences the success of your marketing efforts. This guide provides a comprehensive approach to effectively research and choose affiliate programs that align with your niche, audience, and revenue goals.

1. **Define Your Niche and Audience:**

Before delving into affiliate programs, clearly define your niche and identify your target audience. Understanding your niche helps you pinpoint relevant products or services that resonate with your audience, increasing the likelihood of successful promotions.

2. **Research Affiliate Programs Within Your Niche:**

Conduct thorough research to identify affiliate programs that cater to your niche. Explore affiliate networks, individual merchants, and industry-specific programs. Take note of factors such as commission rates, cookie durations, and the quality of products or services offered.

3. **Explore Reputable Affiliate Networks:**

Consider exploring reputable affiliate networks such as ShareASale, CJ Affiliate, Rakuten Advertising, or others relevant to your niche. Affiliate networks act as intermediaries, offering a consolidated platform to discover and join multiple programs, streamlining your affiliate marketing efforts.

4. Evaluate Merchant Reputation:

Assess the reputation and credibility of merchants associated with the affiliate programs. Consider the quality of their products or services, customer reviews, and the overall standing of the merchant in the industry. Partnering with reputable merchants enhances your credibility as an affiliate.

5. Commission Structures and Payment Terms:

Examine the commission structures offered by affiliate programs. Some programs offer fixed commissions, while others provide tiered structures or performance-based incentives. Additionally, review payment terms, including payout thresholds and frequency, to ensure they align with your financial goals.

6. Cookie Duration Consideration:

Cookie duration is a critical factor in affiliate marketing. Evaluate the cookie duration offered by each program, as it determines the timeframe during which affiliates earn commissions for user actions after clicking their affiliate links. Longer cookie durations provide extended earning opportunities.

7. Affiliate Program Policies and Restrictions:

Thoroughly review the terms and policies of affiliate programs. Pay attention to promotional guidelines, restrictions, and exclusivity clauses. Ensure that the program's policies align with your preferred promotional methods and strategies to avoid conflicts later on.

8. Application Process and Approval Criteria:

Initiate the application process for selected affiliate programs. Provide accurate and detailed information about your promotional methods, audience demographics, and online presence. Be aware of any specific criteria for approval and tailor your application accordingly.

9. Review Affiliate Program Approval:

Upon submitting your application, patiently await approval from the affiliate programs. Approval processes vary, with some programs offering instant approval and others requiring manual review. Be prepared to comply with any additional requests or requirements from the program.

10. Access Affiliate Resources:

Upon approval, access the affiliate dashboard and explore available resources. Most affiliate programs provide promotional materials, tracking tools, and reporting features. Familiarize yourself with these resources to optimize your promotional efforts and track your performance effectively.

11. Diversify Your Affiliate Portfolio:

Consider diversifying your affiliate portfolio by joining multiple programs within your niche. Diversification not only mitigates risks associated with changes in individual programs but also allows you to explore a variety of products or services, catering to diverse audience interests.

12. Assess Program Performance Metrics:

Implement robust tracking mechanisms to monitor the performance of your affiliate marketing efforts. Track key metrics such as clicks, conversions, and commissions using affiliate tracking tools and analytics. Regularly analyze this data to optimize your strategies and focus on high-performing programs.

13. Stay Informed About Program Changes:

Affiliate programs may undergo changes in commission structures, policies, or product offerings. Stay informed about program updates by regularly checking communication channels, newsletters, or announcements from the affiliate programs you are a part of.

14. Evaluate Long-Term Relationship Potential:

Cultivate long-term relationships with affiliate programs and merchants. Consider factors such as ongoing support, communication, and the potential for growth. Building strong relationships contributes to sustained success in the affiliate marketing landscape.

15. Make Informed Selections:

Finally, make informed selections based on the comprehensive research conducted. Choose affiliate programs that not only align with your niche and audience but also offer favorable commission structures, transparent policies, and a positive reputation within the industry.

By diligently researching and selecting affiliate programs, you lay the groundwork for a successful and lucrative affiliate marketing journey. Strategic partnerships with reputable programs enhance your earning potential and contribute to long-term success in the ever-evolving affiliate marketing landscape.

5.2 Best Practices for Joining Affiliate Programs

Joining affiliate programs is a crucial step in establishing a successful affiliate marketing venture. Adhering to best practices ensures that you choose programs aligning with your goals and sets the stage for fruitful collaborations. Here are essential best practices to follow when joining affiliate programs:

1. **Define Your Niche and Audience:**

Clearly define your niche and identify your target audience.

Understanding your niche helps you select relevant affiliate programs that resonate with your audience.

2. **Thoroughly Research Affiliate Programs:**

Conduct extensive research on potential affiliate programs within your niche.

Explore reputable affiliate networks and individual merchants to find programs that align with your content and audience.

3. **Explore Affiliate Networks:**

Consider joining reputable affiliate networks such as ShareASale, CJ Affiliate, or Rakuten Advertising.

Affiliate networks provide a centralized platform to discover and manage multiple affiliate programs efficiently.

4. **Assess Merchant Reputation:**

Evaluate the reputation and credibility of merchants associated with affiliate programs.

Choose programs with reputable merchants to enhance your credibility as an affiliate.

5. Review Commission Structures:

Examine the commission structures offered by affiliate programs.

Look for programs that offer competitive commission rates and align with your revenue goals.

6. Understand Cookie Duration:

Evaluate the cookie duration offered by each program.

Longer cookie durations provide extended earning opportunities, especially for products with longer sales cycles.

7. Familiarize Yourself with Policies:

Thoroughly review the terms and policies of affiliate programs.

Understand promotional guidelines, restrictions, and exclusivity clauses to avoid conflicts later on.

8. Complete the Application Thoughtfully:

Provide accurate and detailed information during the application process.

Tailor your application to meet the specific criteria of each program and showcase your promotional methods.

9.   Patience for Approval Process:

Be patient during the approval process.

Approval timelines vary, with some programs offering instant approval and others requiring manual review.

10.   Access and Explore Affiliate Resources:

- Upon approval, access the affiliate dashboard and explore available resources.

- Familiarize yourself with promotional materials, tracking tools, and reporting features provided by the program.

11. Diversify Your Portfolio:

- Consider diversifying your affiliate portfolio by joining multiple programs.

- Diversification helps mitigate risks associated with changes in individual programs and broadens your earning potential.

12. Monitor Key Performance Metrics:

- Implement tracking mechanisms to monitor key performance metrics.

- Regularly analyze clicks, conversions, and commissions to optimize your strategies and focus on high-performing programs.

13. Stay Informed About Changes:

- Stay informed about changes in commission structures, policies, or product offerings.

- Regularly check communication channels, newsletters, or announcements from the affiliate programs to stay updated.

14. Foster Long-Term Relationships:

- Cultivate long-term relationships with affiliate programs and merchants.

- Consider factors such as ongoing support, communication, and the potential for growth.

15. Choose Programs Strategically:

- Make informed selections based on comprehensive research and evaluation.

- Choose affiliate programs that align with your niche, audience, and overall business objectives.

By following these best practices, you ensure that your journey into affiliate marketing is built on a solid foundation. Strategic affiliations with reputable programs enhance your chances of success and contribute to sustained growth in the competitive landscape of affiliate marketing.

Chapter 6: Maximizing Affiliate Revenue

In the intricate realm of affiliate marketing, the pursuit of maximizing revenue is at the forefront of every affiliate marketer's objectives. This chapter delves into strategic approaches and actionable techniques that empower affiliates to optimize their earning potential, fostering sustainable growth in the dynamic landscape of digital marketing.

1. **Diversifying Product Promotions:**

Expand your revenue streams by diversifying the products or services you promote. Identify complementary products within your niche and strategically integrate them into your content. Offering a variety of options enhances your audience's choices and increases the likelihood of conversions.

2. **Implementing Multi-Channel Marketing:**

Extend your reach by implementing multi-channel marketing strategies. Utilize various platforms, such as social media, email marketing, and your website, to promote affiliate products. Each channel serves as a unique avenue to connect with different segments of your audience, maximizing exposure and potential earnings.

3. **Leveraging Seasonal and Trend-Based Promotions:**

Align your promotions with seasonal trends, holidays, or industry-specific events. Create timely and relevant content that resonates with your audience during peak periods of consumer activity. Leveraging seasonal promotions capitalizes on heightened interest and purchasing behaviors, boosting your affiliate revenue.

4. Implementing Strategic Content Upgrades:

Enhance the value of your content by strategically implementing content upgrades. Offer downloadable guides, templates, or exclusive content in exchange for users clicking on your affiliate links. This tactic not only provides additional value to your audience but also encourages them to take desired actions.

5. Utilizing A/B Testing:

Optimize your promotional strategies through A/B testing. Experiment with different calls-to-action, promotional placements, and content formats to identify what resonates most effectively with your audience. A/B testing enables data-driven decision-making, leading to improved conversion rates and increased revenue.

6. Negotiating Higher Commissions:

Establish strong relationships with merchants and affiliate program managers. Once you've proven your ability to drive quality traffic and sales, consider negotiating for higher commission rates. Demonstrating the value you bring to the partnership can lead to mutually beneficial arrangements that maximize your earning potential.

7. Creating High-Converting Landing Pages:

Design and optimize dedicated landing pages for affiliate promotions. Ensure that these pages are focused, compelling, and tailored to drive conversions. A well-crafted landing page can significantly improve the likelihood of users taking the desired actions, ultimately boosting your affiliate revenue.

8. Building and Nurturing an Email List:

Build an engaged email list and nurture it with valuable content. Use email marketing to promote affiliate products, share exclusive offers, and establish a direct line of communication with your audience. An email list is a powerful asset for driving consistent affiliate revenue.

9. Exploring Upsell Opportunities:

Identify upsell opportunities within affiliate programs. Some merchants offer upsell options during the checkout process, providing an opportunity for affiliates to earn additional commissions. Explore and strategically incorporate upsell opportunities into your promotional efforts.

10. Staying Informed About Industry Trends:

Remain abreast of industry trends and emerging technologies. Being proactive in adapting to changes in consumer behavior and market trends positions you to capitalize on new opportunities. Staying informed allows you to optimize your strategies for maximum affiliate revenue.

11. Continuous Optimization with Analytics:

Regularly analyze performance metrics using analytics tools. Monitor key indicators such as click-through rates, conversion rates, and earnings. Identify trends, understand user behavior, and use data-driven insights to continuously optimize your affiliate marketing strategies for improved revenue generation.

12. Engaging in Limited-Time Promotions:

Create a sense of urgency by incorporating limited-time promotions. Communicate exclusive deals, discounts, or bonuses that are time-sensitive. Limited-time offers compel users to take immediate action, driving conversions and maximizing affiliate revenue during promotional periods.

13. Incorporating User-Generated Content:

Encourage and leverage user-generated content (UGC) in your promotions. User testimonials, reviews, and shared experiences add authenticity to your recommendations. Incorporating UGC can enhance trust, increase engagement, and ultimately contribute to higher conversion rates and affiliate revenue.

14. Scaling Successful Campaigns:

Identify your most successful affiliate marketing campaigns and scale them. Analyze the elements that contributed to their success and replicate those strategies in new campaigns. Scaling successful campaigns allows you to capitalize on proven methods and maximize your overall affiliate revenue.

15. Staying Adaptable to Market Dynamics:

The digital landscape evolves, and market dynamics change. Stay adaptable by continually reassessing your strategies in response to shifts in consumer behavior, technology, and industry trends. Flexibility and adaptability are key to maintaining and maximizing affiliate revenue over the long term.

By integrating these strategies into your affiliate marketing approach, you can position yourself for sustained success and maximize your revenue potential. The dynamic nature of the digital landscape provides ample opportunities for affiliates who are strategic, adaptive and committed to delivering value to their audience.

6.1 Effective Promotion Techniques

In the competitive landscape of affiliate marketing, the success of your promotional efforts hinges on employing effective techniques that capture the attention of your audience and drive desired actions. Here are proven promotion techniques to enhance your affiliate marketing strategy:

1. **Compelling Content Creation:**

Develop high-quality and valuable content that resonates with your audience.

Craft engaging blog posts, articles, product reviews, and multimedia content to showcase the benefits of the affiliate products you promote.

2. **Strategic Use of Social Media:**

Leverage the power of social media platforms to expand your reach.

Share affiliate promotions through well-crafted posts, images, and videos. Engage with your audience, respond to comments, and utilize relevant hashtags to increase visibility.

3. **Email Marketing Campaigns:**

Build and nurture an email list to establish direct communication with your audience.

Implement targeted email marketing campaigns to promote affiliate products, share exclusive offers, and provide valuable content to your subscribers.

4. SEO Optimization:

Optimize your content for search engines to improve organic visibility.

Conduct keyword research, optimize Meta tags, and focus on creating content that addresses the needs and queries of your target audience.

5. Influencer Collaborations:

Collaborate with influencers in your niche to extend your reach.

Influencers can introduce your affiliate products to their audience, leveraging their credibility and expanding your promotional reach.

6. Interactive and Engaging Content:

Incorporate interactive elements into your content.

Use polls, quizzes, surveys, and other interactive features to engage your audience and encourage participation.

7. Limited-Time Promotions:

Create a sense of urgency with limited-time promotions.

Communicate exclusive deals, discounts, or bonuses that are time-sensitive, compelling users to take immediate action.

8. Utilizing Paid Advertising:

Consider using paid advertising channels to amplify your reach.

Platforms like Facebook Ads, Google Ads, and native advertising can help target specific demographics and reach a broader audience.

9. Webinars and Live Events:

Host webinars or live events to showcase and discuss affiliate products.

Interact directly with your audience, addressing their questions and concerns in real time.

10. Native Advertising:

- Blend affiliate promotions seamlessly into your content with native advertising.

- Craft promotional content that aligns with the natural flow of your platform, enhancing user experience.

11. Comparison and Review Articles:

- Create comparison and review articles to help users make informed decisions.

- Provide comprehensive and unbiased information about affiliate products, highlighting their features, benefits, and potential drawbacks.

12. Retargeting Campaigns:

- Implement retargeting campaigns to reach users who have previously engaged with your content.

- Remind them of the affiliate products they viewed, increasing the likelihood of conversion.

13. Social Proof and Testimonials:

- Showcase social proof and user testimonials.

- Highlight positive experiences and testimonials from users who have benefited from the affiliate products you're promoting.

14. Podcast Sponsorships:

- Explore podcast sponsorships to reach a targeted audience.

- Collaborate with podcast creators in your niche for sponsored content or shout-outs.

15. Gamification Strategies:

- Incorporate gamification elements into your promotions.

- Create contests, challenges, or interactive games to encourage user participation and increase engagement.

16. Mobile Optimization:

- Ensure your content and promotions are optimized for mobile devices.

- With a growing number of users accessing content on mobile, mobile optimization is essential for reaching a broader audience.

17. Cross-Promotion with Affiliates:

- Collaborate with other affiliates in your niche for cross-promotion.

- Share each other's content or run joint promotions to tap into each other's audiences.

18. Educational Resources and Tutorials:

- Create educational resources and tutorials related to affiliate products.

- Position yourself as an authority in your niche by providing valuable information that addresses your audience's needs.

19. Targeted Landing Pages:

- Design targeted landing pages for specific affiliate promotions.

- Ensure that landing pages are optimized for conversions and provide a clear call-to-action.

20. Continuous Testing and Optimization:

- Continuously test and optimize your promotional strategies.

- Analyze data, track performance metrics, and refine your approach based on what resonates most effectively with your audience.

By incorporating these effective promotion techniques into your affiliate marketing strategy, you can create a dynamic and engaging promotional plan that maximizes your reach, engages your audience, and drives conversions for the affiliate products you promote.

6.2 Optimizing Conversion Rates

In the realm of affiliate marketing, the pursuit of higher conversion rates is a cornerstone for success. The ability to turn visitors into active customers directly impacts your affiliate revenue. Implementing strategic tactics to optimize conversion rates is essential. Here's a comprehensive guide to help you boost conversions effectively:

1. **Understanding Your Audience:**

Develop a deep understanding of your target audience, their preferences, and pain points.

Tailor your messaging and promotional strategies to resonate with your audience's needs and motivations.

2. **Compelling Call-to-Action (CTA):**

Craft clear and compelling CTAs that prompt immediate action.

Use persuasive language and create a sense of urgency to encourage visitors to click on your affiliate links.

3. **A/B Testing:**

Conduct A/B testing on various elements of your promotions.

Test different headlines, CTAs, images, and layouts to identify the most effective combinations that drive higher conversion rates.

4. **Streamlined User Experience:**

Ensure a seamless and user-friendly experience on your website or platform.

Streamline navigation, minimize page load times, and optimize the layout for easy access to affiliate links and product information.

5. Trust-Building Elements:

Incorporate trust-building elements to enhance credibility.

Display trust badges, customer testimonials, and recognizable affiliations to instill confidence in your audience.

6. Compelling Content:

Create engaging and informative content around the affiliate products.

Clearly communicate the value and benefits of the products to help visitors make informed decisions.

7. Personalization:

Implement personalized experiences for your audience.

Use data to tailor content, recommendations, and offers based on individual preferences and behavior.

8. Responsive Design:

Ensure your website or landing pages are optimized for various devices.

Responsive design ensures a consistent and user-friendly experience across desktops, tablets, and mobile devices.

9. Limited-Time Offers:

Introduce limited-time offers or exclusive deals to create a sense of urgency.

Limited-time promotions can drive immediate action from visitors who fear missing out on special opportunities.

10. Clear Value Proposition:

- Clearly communicate the unique value proposition of the affiliate products.

- Highlight key features, benefits, and any exclusive advantages users gain by taking action through your affiliate links.

11. Exit-Intent Popups:

- Use exit-intent popups to capture visitors who are about to leave.

- Present special offers or incentives to encourage them to reconsider and take the desired action.

12. Optimized Landing Pages:

- Design dedicated landing pages optimized for conversions.

- Remove distractions, provide concise information, and guide visitors toward the desired action.

13. Social Proof:

- Showcase social proof through reviews, testimonials, and user success stories.

- Authentic experiences from others build trust and credibility, influencing conversion decisions.

14. Transparent Affiliate Disclosure:

- Clearly disclose your affiliate relationships to build trust.

- Transparently communicate that you may earn a commission, fostering honesty and integrity with your audience.

15. Strategic Placement of Affiliate Links:

- Place affiliate links strategically within your content.

- Ensure links are prominently visible, relevant, and seamlessly integrated into the flow of your content.

16. Targeted and Relevant Messaging:

- Tailor your messaging to match the specific interests of your audience.

- Speak directly to their pain points, desires, and motivations, creating a more personalized connection.

17. Implementing Retargeting Strategies:

- Utilize retargeting to re-engage visitors who didn't convert initially.

- Display targeted ads or offers to bring them back to your affiliate promotions.

18. Offer Incentives:

- Provide additional incentives, such as bonuses or exclusive discounts, for users who convert through your affiliate links.

- Extra perks can sway users towards taking the desired action.

19. Data Analysis and Iteration:

- Regularly analyze conversion data using analytics tools.

- Use insights to identify patterns, understand user behavior, and make iterative improvements to your conversion strategy.

20. Interactive and Multimedia Elements:

- Integrate interactive elements and multimedia content to enhance engagement.

- Videos, interactive graphics, and quizzes can captivate visitors and drive them towards conversion.

By implementing these strategies and continually refining your approach based on data-driven insights, you can optimize conversion rates and elevate the effectiveness of your affiliate marketing efforts. Consistent testing, user-focused strategies, and a commitment to providing value are key components in the journey to maximizing your affiliate conversion rates.

Chapter 7: Overcoming Challenges in Affiliate Marketing

In the dynamic landscape of affiliate marketing, success is often accompanied by various challenges that require strategic navigation. This chapter explores common hurdles faced by affiliate marketers and provides actionable insights to overcome them, ensuring a resilient and thriving affiliate marketing journey.

1. Adapting to Market Saturation:

Challenge: Saturation in certain niches can lead to increased competition and difficulty in standing out.

Solution: Differentiate your approach by offering unique value, targeting untapped sub-niches, or presenting familiar products in innovative ways. Emphasize your personal brand and establish a distinctive voice to capture audience's attention.

2. Navigating Regulatory Compliance:

Challenge: Adherence to ever-changing legal and regulatory requirements poses a challenge for affiliate marketers.

Solution: Stay informed about industry regulations, particularly in areas like disclosure and data privacy. Clearly communicate your affiliate relationships, and consider consulting legal professionals to ensure compliance with regional and industry-specific laws.

3. Building Credibility and Trust:

Challenge: Establishing trust with your audience can be challenging, especially in an environment where skepticism prevails.

Solution: Prioritize transparency and authenticity in your communications. Provide valuable, unbiased content, share personal experiences, and showcase social proof through testimonials and reviews. Consistently delivering quality content builds credibility over time.

4. Managing Affiliate Program Changes:

Challenge: Affiliate programs may undergo alterations in commission structures, policies, or product offerings.

Solution: Stay vigilant by regularly checking program updates and communications. Diversify your portfolio to minimize the impact of changes in any single program. Cultivate relationships with program managers to stay informed and adapt your strategy accordingly.

5. Dealing with Platform Algorithm Changes:

Challenge: Changes in search engine algorithms or social media platforms can affect the visibility of your content.

Solution: Stay updated on algorithm changes through industry news and official updates. Focus on creating high-quality, user-centric content that aligns with the platform's guidelines. Diversify your traffic sources to reduce reliance on a single channel.

6. Balancing Quantity and Quality:

Challenge: Striking the right balance between producing a high volume of content and maintaining quality can be demanding.

Solution: Prioritize quality over quantity. Focus on creating in-depth, valuable content that addresses the needs of your audience. Implement efficient content creation workflows and consider outsourcing or repurposing content to maintain consistency.

7. Adapting to Technological Advancements:

Challenge: Rapid technological advancements may require continuous adaptation to new tools and platforms.

Solution: Stay informed about emerging technologies relevant to affiliate marketing. Embrace automation, analytics tools, and other innovations to streamline processes and enhance your marketing strategy. Continuously invest in learning to stay ahead.

8. Handling Payment and Commission Issues:

Challenge: Late payments, tracking discrepancies, or commission-related challenges can arise.

Solution: Choose reputable affiliate programs with transparent payment terms. Regularly monitor your affiliate dashboard for accurate tracking. Establish open communication with affiliate managers to address payment or commission concerns promptly.

9. Overcoming Content Burnout:

Challenge: Consistently producing engaging content can lead to burnout over time.

Solution: Implement a content calendar with realistic timelines. Explore different content formats, collaborate with others, and repurpose existing content. Take breaks to recharge creatively and maintain a healthy work-life balance.

10. Adhering to Ethical Practices:

- Challenge: Ethical concerns may arise, particularly in promoting products or services that may not align with your values or those of your audience.

- Solution: Prioritize ethical considerations in your affiliate partnerships. Only promote products or services you genuinely believe in. Clearly disclose affiliate relationships to maintain transparency with your audience.

11. Embracing Continuous Learning:

- Challenge: Staying updated on industry trends and best practices requires ongoing education.

- Solution: Dedicate time to continuous learning through industry publications, online courses, webinars, and networking with fellow affiliate marketers. Stay curious and open to adapting your strategies based on new insights.

12. Resilience in the Face of Setbacks:

- Challenge: Setbacks, whether in the form of unsuccessful campaigns or external challenges, can be demotivating.

- Solution: Cultivate resilience by viewing setbacks as opportunities to learn and improve. Analyze the factors contributing to challenges, adapt your strategy, and maintain a positive mindset. Networking with peers can provide valuable support during challenging times.

Navigating the challenges of affiliate marketing requires a combination of strategic thinking, adaptability, and a commitment to ethical and transparent practices. By addressing these challenges head-on, affiliate marketers can position themselves for long-term success in this ever-evolving industry.

7.1 Dealing with Saturation and Competition

In the competitive landscape of affiliate marketing, dealing with saturation and heightened competition is a common challenge. As more affiliates enter popular niches, standing out and capturing the attention of your target audience becomes increasingly demanding. Here are strategies to effectively navigate saturation and competition in the affiliate marketing space:

1. Niche Specialization:

Approach: Focus on a specific sub-niche or a unique angle within a broader category.

Why: Specializing allows you to become an authority in a particular area, making it easier to differentiate yourself and attract a dedicated audience interested in specific aspects of the niche.

2. Unique Value Proposition (UVP):

Approach: Clearly define and communicate what sets you apart from other affiliates.

Why: A compelling UVP helps you stand out in a crowded market. Emphasize what makes your approach, content, or recommendations unique and valuable to your audience.

3. In-Depth and Quality Content:

Approach: Prioritize creating comprehensive, high-quality content that goes beyond surface-level information.

Why: In-depth content not only demonstrates expertise but also provides more value to your audience. This can contribute to higher rankings in search engines and increased credibility.

4. Target Long-Tail Keywords:

Approach: Optimize your content for long-tail keywords related to your niche.

Why: Long-tail keywords are specific and often have less competition. Targeting them can help your content rank higher in search results, attracting a more targeted audience.

5. Build a Personal Brand:

Approach: Develop and showcase your unique personality, voice, and style across your platforms.

Why: Building a personal brand fosters a connection with your audience. People are more likely to engage with content that feels authentic and aligns with their preferences.

6. Diversify Traffic Sources:

Approach: Explore multiple channels for driving traffic, such as social media, email marketing, and paid advertising.

Why: Relying on a single source for traffic makes you vulnerable to changes in algorithms or market dynamics. Diversification spreads risk and ensures a more stable audience acquisition strategy.

7. Collaborate with Other Affiliates:

Approach: Form partnerships or collaborations with other affiliates in your niche.

Why: Collaborations can expand your reach by tapping into each other's audiences. Joint promotions, content swaps, or co-created projects can offer mutual benefits.

8. Stay Updated on Trends:

Approach: Regularly research and stay informed about emerging trends in your niche.

Why: Being aware of industry trends allows you to adapt your content and strategies accordingly. It positions you as an informed and relevant source for your audience.

9. Utilize Paid Advertising Strategically:

Approach: Incorporate paid advertising into your strategy, focusing on targeted campaigns.

Why: Paid advertising can help amplify your reach and target specific audience segments. Strategic ad campaigns can complement organic efforts and increase visibility.

10. Engage with Your Audience:

- Approach: Actively engage with your audience through comments, social media, and email.

- Why: Building a community around your content fosters loyalty. Responding to comments and messages helps create a connection, making your audience more likely to trust your recommendations.

11. Offer Exclusive Content or Bonuses:

- Approach: Provide exclusive content, bonuses, or offers to your audience.

- Why: Exclusive content or bonuses incentivize users to choose your affiliate links over others. It adds extra value and encourages conversions.

12. Monitor Competitor Strategies:

- Approach: Keep an eye on what other affiliates in your niche are doing.

- Why: Monitoring competitors allows you to identify gaps in the market, discover new opportunities, and adapt your strategies based on successful approaches.

13. Continuous Learning and Adaptation:

- Approach: Commit to ongoing learning and adapt your strategies based on industry changes.

- Why: The affiliate marketing landscape evolves. Staying informed and adaptable positions you to navigate shifts in competition, technology, and consumer behavior.

By implementing these strategies, you can effectively navigate saturation and competition in affiliate marketing. Building a unique and authentic presence, providing valuable content, and staying attuned to industry trends are essential elements in establishing a successful and resilient affiliate marketing strategy.

7.2 Adapting to Industry Changes

In the dynamic realm of affiliate marketing, staying ahead of industry changes is crucial for maintaining relevance and achieving sustained success. The landscape evolves rapidly, influenced by technological advancements, shifts in consumer behavior, and updates to search engine algorithms. Here are key strategies to effectively adapt to industry changes in affiliate marketing:

1. **Stay Informed and Engage in Continuous Learning:**

Approach: Regularly consume industry publications, attend webinars, and participate in forums or communities.

Why: Staying informed about the latest trends, updates, and best practices equips you with the knowledge needed to adapt your strategies to changing dynamics.

2. Monitor Algorithm Updates:

Approach: Keep a close eye on updates from major search engines and social media platforms.

Why: Algorithm changes can significantly impact the visibility of your content. Understanding and adapting to these updates ensures that your content remains optimized for current ranking criteria.

3. Embrace New Technologies:

Approach: Explore and adopt emerging technologies relevant to affiliate marketing.

Why: Innovations such as AI, automation tools, and new advertising platforms can enhance efficiency and effectiveness. Embracing technological advancements allows you to stay competitive and leverage new opportunities.

4. Diversify Traffic Sources:

Approach: Avoid overreliance on a single traffic source; diversify across platforms.

Why: Changes in algorithms or policies on one platform can impact your traffic. Diversification spreads risk and ensures that your audience can be reached through multiple channels.

5.   Adapt Content Strategies:

Approach: Analyze shifts in content consumption habits and adjust your content strategies accordingly.

Why: Changes in how users consume content, such as the rise of video or the popularity of certain formats, should influence your content creation approach. Stay adaptable to emerging content trends.

6.   Regularly Assess and Update SEO Practices:

Approach: Continuously evaluate and adjust your SEO strategies in response to algorithm changes.

Why: SEO is integral to affiliate marketing success. Regular updates to SEO practices, including keyword optimization and on-page SEO, ensure that your content remains visible in search engine results.

7.   Evaluate Affiliate Program Changes:

Approach: Regularly review updates and changes in the affiliate programs you participate in.

Why: Affiliate programs may alter commission structures, terms, or policies. Staying informed allows you to adapt your promotional strategies and focus on programs that align with your goals.

8.   Analyze Consumer Behavior:

Approach: Monitor changes in consumer behavior and preferences.

Why: Understanding how your target audience interacts with online content, and shops, and makes decisions is crucial. Adapt your strategies to meet evolving consumer expectations.

9. Leverage Data Analytics:

Approach: Utilize analytics tools to gather and analyze performance data.

Why: Data-driven insights provide valuable feedback on the effectiveness of your strategies. Analyze key performance indicators to identify trends, opportunities, and areas for improvement.

10. Engage in Networking and Collaboration:

- Approach: Build and maintain connections within the affiliate marketing community.

- Why: Networking allows you to exchange insights, learn from others' experiences, and stay attuned to industry shifts. Collaborations with peers can provide fresh perspectives and new opportunities.

11. Adapt to Regulatory Changes:

- Approach: Stay informed about changes in legal and regulatory frameworks affecting affiliate marketing.

- Why: Compliance is essential for long-term success. Adapting to new regulations ensures that your strategies remain ethical and align with legal requirements.

12. Test and Experiment:

- Approach: Implement controlled tests and experiments to assess the impact of changes in your strategies.

- Why: Testing allows you to measure the effectiveness of adjustments in a controlled environment. Experimentation helps you identify what works best for your specific audience and niche.

13. Seek Feedback from Your Audience:

- Approach: Encourage feedback from your audience through surveys, comments, or social media interactions.

- Why: Direct feedback provides valuable insights into how your audience perceives and engages with your content. Use this information to make informed adjustments.

Adapting to industry changes in affiliate marketing requires a proactive and strategic approach. By staying informed, embracing new technologies, diversifying your strategies, and engaging with the affiliate marketing community, you position yourself for sustained success in the ever-evolving landscape of digital marketing.

Chapter 8: Scaling Your Affiliate Business

Scaling an affiliate business involves strategic expansion, optimization, and leveraging proven tactics to increase reach and profitability. In this chapter, we'll explore actionable steps and key considerations to guide you in scaling your affiliate business successfully.

1. **Assessing Current Performance:**

Overview: Before scaling, conduct a thorough assessment of your current affiliate business performance.

Action Steps:

- Analyze key performance indicators (KPIs) such as conversion rates, click-through rates, and earnings.
- Identify high-performing products, content, and traffic sources.
- Evaluate the scalability of your current strategies.

2. **Identifying Growth Opportunities:**

Overview: Uncover untapped opportunities for growth within your niche and beyond.

Action Steps:

- Research emerging trends in your niche.
- Explore related niches or sub-niches for potential expansion.
- Identify complementary products or services to promote.

3. Diversifying Product Offerings:

Overview: Expand your affiliate portfolio by diversifying the products you promote.

Action Steps:

- Research and join new affiliate programs.
- Identify high-converting products with relevance to your audience.
- Ensure diversity to mitigate risks associated with fluctuations in individual products.

4. Scaling Content Production:

Overview: Increase the quantity and quality of your content to reach a broader audience.

Action Steps:

- Implement content calendars for consistent publishing.

- Explore various content formats, including videos, podcasts, and infographics.
- Outsource or hire additional resources for content creation if necessary.

5. Expanding Traffic Sources:

Overview: Broaden your reach by exploring new and diverse traffic sources.

Action Steps:

- Invest in paid advertising on platforms relevant to your audience.
- Explore influencer collaborations to tap into established audiences.
- Optimize your content for additional search engine visibility.

6. Building Email Marketing Sequences:

Overview: Develop and optimize email marketing campaigns to nurture and convert leads.

Action Steps:

- Build and segment your email list for targeted communication.

- Create automated sequences for onboarding, promotions, and engagement.
- Test and optimize email campaigns for maximum effectiveness.

7. Implementing Automation Tools:

Overview: Streamline processes and workflows through the integration of automation tools.

Action Steps:

- Utilize tools for social media scheduling, email marketing, and analytics.
- Explore affiliate marketing platforms with automation features.
- Identify repetitive tasks that can be automated for increased efficiency.

8. Forming Strategic Partnerships:

Overview: Collaborate with other businesses, influencers, or affiliates to amplify your reach.

Action Steps:

- Identify potential partners with aligned values and audience demographics.
- Propose mutually beneficial collaborations, such as joint promotions.
- Leverage partnerships to access new audiences and enhance credibility.

9. **Scaling Paid Advertising Campaigns:**

Overview: Increase the budget and scope of your paid advertising efforts.

Action Steps:

- Identify high-converting keywords and audiences for paid search and social campaigns.
- Set realistic budgets for scaling without compromising ROI.
- Monitor and adjust ad campaigns based on performance data.

10. **Optimizing Conversion Funnels:**

Overview: Fine-tune your conversion funnels for increased efficiency.

Action Steps:

- Analyze user journeys and identify potential points of friction.
- Implement A/B testing for landing pages and CTAs.
- Optimize the checkout process for improved conversion rates.

11. Investing in Scalable Technologies:

Overview: Upgrade your technological infrastructure to support scalability.

Action Steps:

- Invest in a reliable hosting solution to handle increased traffic.
- Consider advanced analytics tools for in-depth performance insights.
- Ensure your website or platform is mobile-friendly and optimized for user experience.

12. Monitoring and Iterating:

Overview: Continuously monitor performance metrics and iterate based on data.

Action Steps:

- Set up regular reviews of key performance indicators.

- Solicit user feedback to identify areas for improvement.
- Iterate on successful strategies while addressing underperforming areas.

13. Establishing Key Performance Indicators (KPIs):

Overview: Define clear KPIs to measure the success of your scaling efforts.

Action Steps:

- Identify quantitative and qualitative metrics aligned with your business goals.
- Regularly assess and adjust KPIs based on evolving business priorities.
- Use KPIs to guide decision-making and resource allocation.

14. Cultivating a Scalable Mindset:

Overview: Foster a mindset that embraces growth, innovation, and adaptability.

Action Steps:

- Encourage a culture of experimentation and learning within your team.
- Embrace failures as learning opportunities and iterate on strategies.
- Celebrate successes and milestones to maintain motivation.

Scaling your affiliate business requires a strategic approach, a commitment to ongoing improvement, and the ability to adapt to changing market dynamics. By implementing these actionable steps and maintaining a focus on sustainable growth, you can successfully scale your affiliate business in the ever-evolving digital landscape.

8.1 Automation and Outsourcing

In the dynamic and time-sensitive world of affiliate marketing, leveraging automation and outsourcing can significantly enhance efficiency, allowing you to focus on strategic aspects of your business. Here's an exploration of how to effectively integrate automation and outsourcing into your affiliate marketing endeavors:

1. **Automation Tools in Affiliate Marketing:**

Overview: Automation tools streamline repetitive tasks, enhance productivity, and provide valuable insights.

Implementation:

- Utilize social media scheduling tools to plan and automate content distribution.
- Employ email marketing automation for personalized and timely communication with your audience.
- Explore tools that automate data analytics, providing insights into performance metrics and user behavior.
- Use affiliate marketing platforms that offer automation features, such as commission tracking and reporting.

2. Content Creation and Outsourcing:

Overview: Outsourcing content creation allows you to scale your content production efficiently.

Implementation:

- Identify tasks suitable for outsourcing, such as blog writing, graphic design, or video production.
- Utilize freelance platforms to find skilled writers, designers, and content creators.
- Clearly communicate your brand voice, style, and requirements to maintain consistency.
- Establish a reliable workflow for content submission, review, and publication.

3. Social Media Automation:

Overview: Automating social media tasks enhances your presence across platforms and engages your audience consistently.

Implementation:

- Schedule posts in advance using social media management tools.
- Set up automated responses for common queries or interactions.
- Utilize social listening tools to monitor mentions and trends in your niche.
- Implement chatbots for instant responses on messaging platforms.

4. **Email Marketing Automation:**

Overview: Automating email campaigns allows for personalized and timely communication with your audience.

Implementation:

- Segment your email list based on user behavior, demographics, or preferences.
- Set up automated sequences for onboarding, promotions, and follow-ups.
- Implement dynamic content that adapts based on user interactions.
- Utilize A/B testing to optimize subject lines, content, and calls to action.

5.   Affiliate Program Management Automation:

Overview: Automate aspects of your affiliate program management for seamless operations.

Implementation:

- Choose affiliate marketing platforms that offer automation features for tracking commissions, generating reports, and managing affiliates.
- Implement automated affiliate onboarding and approval processes.
- Set up automatic notifications for affiliates regarding promotions, updates, or policy changes.
- Utilize automated affiliate payout systems for timely and accurate payments.

6.   SEO Automation Tools:

Overview: Automate certain aspects of search engine optimization (SEO) to improve your website's visibility.

Implementation:

- Use SEO tools for keyword research, rank tracking, and competitor analysis.

- Implement automated SEO audits to identify and address website issues.
- Utilize plugins or tools for automated metadata optimization.
- Set up alerts for changes in search engine algorithms to adapt your strategy proactively.

7. **Data Analysis Automation:**

Overview: Automate the collection and analysis of data to inform your decision-making process.

Implementation:

- Utilize data analytics tools to automatically gather and consolidate performance metrics.
- Implement machine learning algorithms for predictive analytics and user behavior analysis.
- Set up automated reports for regular performance reviews.
- Utilize dashboards that offer real-time insights into key performance indicators.

8. **Customer Relationship Management (CRM) Automation:**

Overview: Automate aspects of customer relationship management to enhance user experience.

Implementation:

- Implement CRM software to automate lead nurturing and customer segmentation.
- Set up automated responses for customer inquiries and support tickets.
- Utilize CRM automation for personalized communication based on customer interactions.
- Implement automated surveys for feedback and insights.

9. Outsourcing Strategy:

Overview: Outsourcing specific tasks allows you to focus on core aspects of your affiliate business.

Implementation:

- Identify tasks that don't require your direct involvement, such as customer support, data entry, or routine administrative work.
- Utilize outsourcing platforms to find qualified professionals or agencies.
- Clearly communicate expectations, provide detailed guidelines, and establish key performance indicators for outsourced tasks.
- Regularly evaluate the performance of outsourced tasks and provide feedback for improvement.

10. Continuous Monitoring and Optimization:

Overview: Regularly monitor the performance of automated processes and outsourced tasks to ensure efficiency.

Implementation:

- Set up alerts for potential issues or anomalies in automated processes.
- Conduct periodic reviews of outsourced tasks to ensure alignment with your business goals.
- Iterate and optimize automated workflows based on performance data.
- Seek feedback from your team and outsourced partners for continuous improvement.

Integrating automation and outsourcing strategically into your affiliate marketing endeavors empowers you to operate more efficiently, scale your business, and focus on the creative and strategic elements that drive success. By embracing these tools and approaches, you can optimize your workflow, enhance productivity, and navigate the ever-evolving landscape of affiliate marketing with agility and effectiveness.

8.2 Diversifying Your Income Streams

In the dynamic landscape of affiliate marketing, diversifying income streams is a key strategy for building resilience, maximizing revenue, and mitigating risks associated with dependency on a single source. Here's a comprehensive guide on how to effectively diversify your income streams within the realm of affiliate marketing:

1. **Multi-Niche Affiliate Marketing:**

Approach: Expand your reach by operating in multiple niches or sub-niches.

Why: Diversifying across different niches minimizes the impact of market fluctuations in any single area. Identify complementary niches that align with your expertise and audience.

2. **Joining Multiple Affiliate Programs:**

Approach: Participate in diverse affiliate programs that offer products or services relevant to your audience.

Why: Relying on multiple affiliate programs spreads the risk associated with changes in commission structures, product availability, or program policies. Choose programs that align with different aspects of your content.

3. **Incorporating Different Content Formats:**

Approach: Diversify your content by incorporating various formats such as blog posts, videos, podcasts, and infographics.

Why: Different audience segments prefer consuming content in different ways. Offering a variety of formats enhances your ability to connect with a broader audience and accommodates diverse preferences.

4. Affiliate Marketing on Various Platforms:

Approach: Extend your affiliate marketing efforts across different online platforms.

Why: Diversifying your presence on platforms like social media, YouTube, or podcast platforms ensures that your content reaches audiences beyond a single channel. Adapt your strategy to each platform's unique characteristics.

5. Building an Email Subscriber List:

Approach: Develop and nurture an email subscriber list for direct communication with your audience.

Why: An email list provides a direct channel to engage with your audience, promote affiliate products, and share exclusive offers. It serves as an independent asset that is not reliant on external platforms.

6. Creating and Selling Digital Products:

Approach: Develop and sell your digital products, such as ebooks, online courses, or templates.

Why: Selling digital products diversifies your revenue streams and allows you to leverage your expertise. It also provides an opportunity for recurring income through memberships or subscriptions.

7. Offering Consultation or Coaching Services:

Approach: Provide consultation or coaching services related to your niche or expertise.

Why: Offering personalized services not only generates additional income but also establishes you as an authority in your field. Consultation services can complement your affiliate marketing efforts.

8. Creating Merchandise or Merchandising Affiliation:

Approach: Develop and sell branded merchandise or collaborate with existing brands for merchandising affiliations.

Why: Merchandising provides an additional revenue stream and allows your audience to support you directly. It also strengthens your brand presence.

9. Sponsored Content and Partnerships:

Approach: Collaborate with brands for sponsored content or partnerships.

Why: Sponsored content provides an alternative income source while allowing you to promote products or services directly. Ensure that partnerships align with your brand and provide value to your audience.

10. Implementing Paid Memberships or Subscriptions:

Approach: Introduce paid membership or subscription models for exclusive content or perks.

Why: Offering premium content or benefits for a subscription fee provides a recurring income stream. It fosters a sense of community among your audience.

11. Affiliate Marketing Events or Webinars:

Approach: Host events, webinars, or online workshops featuring affiliate products or services.

Why: Live events offer opportunities for direct engagement and can serve as additional revenue streams through ticket sales, sponsorships, or affiliate commissions.

12. Monetizing Your Social Media Presence:

Approach: Monetize your social media presence through sponsored posts, affiliate links, or exclusive content for subscribers.

Why: Social media platforms offer diverse monetization opportunities. Utilize features like Instagram Shoppable posts or Facebook Shops to directly monetize your audience.

13. Incorporating E-commerce and Dropshipping:

Approach: Integrate e-commerce or dropshipping into your affiliate marketing strategy.

Why: Selling physical products through e-commerce or dropshipping provides an additional income stream. Carefully select products that complement your niche.

14. Real Estate and Property Affiliation:

Approach: Explore affiliate programs related to real estate, property management, or home-related services.

Why: Real estate affiliations provide a unique avenue for generating income, especially if your audience is interested in homeownership or property investment.

15. Cryptocurrency and Finance Affiliation:

Approach: Explore affiliations related to cryptocurrency, fintech, or personal finance.

Why: The finance niche offers diverse opportunities for affiliate marketing. Explore partnerships with platforms offering financial tools, investment products, or cryptocurrency services.

16. Collaborating with Influencers or Cross-Promotions:

Approach: Collaborate with influencers or businesses for cross-promotions.

Why: Partnering with influencers expands your reach to their audience, introducing your content and affiliate promotions to a new set of potential customers.

17. Affiliate Marketing Workshops or Courses:

Approach: Offer workshops or courses on affiliate marketing best practices.

Why: Sharing your knowledge through educational content not only generates income but also positions you as an expert in affiliate marketing.

18. Implementing Loyalty Programs:

Approach: Introduce loyalty programs or reward systems for your audience.

Why: Loyalty programs incentivize repeat business and encourage your audience to continue engaging with your content and affiliate promotions.

19. Adapting to Emerging Trends:

Approach: Stay informed about emerging trends and technologies in your niche.

Why: Being adaptable and staying ahead of trends allows you to identify new income opportunities early on. Embrace innovations that align with your audience's evolving needs.

20. Regularly Assessing and Adapting Strategies:

Approach: Continuously assess the performance of each income stream and adapt your strategies accordingly.

Why: Regular evaluations ensure that your diversified income streams remain aligned with your goals. Identify underperforming areas and explore new opportunities for growth.

By diversifying your income streams, you not only safeguard your affiliate marketing business against uncertainties but also unlock new avenues for growth and innovation. Embrace a strategic and adaptive mindset as you explore these diverse income streams, and tailor your approach to align with the evolving needs and preferences of your audience.

Chapter 9: Case Studies

In this chapter, we delve into real-world case studies that illustrate the application of affiliate marketing strategies and showcase successful outcomes. Each case study provides valuable insights, lessons learned, and practical takeaways that can inform and inspire your own affiliate marketing journey.

Case Study 1: Niche Domination in Health and Wellness

Overview: Explore how a content creator achieved niche domination in the competitive health and wellness space.

Strategies:

- In-depth Content: The affiliate consistently produced comprehensive, well-researched content, establishing authority in the niche.
- Strategic Product Selection: Focused on promoting high-quality products aligned with audience needs and preferences.
- Engagement Tactics: Actively engaged with the audience through comments, social media, and newsletters.
- Outcomes: Significant growth in organic traffic, increased affiliate revenue, and a loyal community.

Case Study 2: Diversification through Multi-Platform Presence

Overview: Explore how an affiliate marketer successfully diversified income streams through a multi-platform approach.

Strategies:

- Platform Diversification: Expanded presence across social media, YouTube, and a dedicated blog.
- Cross-Promotions: Collaborated with influencers for cross-promotions, reaching new audiences.
- Adaptation to Trends: Stayed informed about emerging trends and adapted content accordingly.
- Outcomes: Increased affiliate revenue from diverse channels, enhanced brand visibility, and resilience against platform changes.

Case Study 3: Monetizing a Personal Brand

Overview: Discover how an individual successfully monetized their personal brand through affiliate marketing.

Strategies:

- Authenticity: Built a personal brand based on authenticity and transparency.

- Exclusive Offers: Negotiated exclusive offers and bonuses for the audience.
- Email Marketing: Leveraged a robust email list for targeted promotions and communication.
- Outcomes: Generated substantial income through affiliate promotions, increased brand loyalty, and opportunities for sponsored collaborations.

Case Study 4: Global Affiliate Campaign Success

Overview: Explore the success of an affiliate marketing campaign targeting a global audience.

Strategies:

- Localization: Adapted content and promotions to resonate with diverse cultural preferences.
- Multilingual Content: Created content in multiple languages to cater to a global audience.
- Time Zone Optimization: Scheduled promotions to align with peak times in different regions.
- Outcomes: Increased conversions from international audiences, expanded affiliate network, and improved brand recognition globally.

Case Study 5: Adapting to Regulatory Changes

Overview: Learn how an affiliate marketer successfully navigated and adapted to changes in regulatory frameworks.

Strategies:

- Legal Compliance: Stayed informed about new regulations and adjusted promotional strategies accordingly.
- Transparent Communication: Communicated openly with the audience about changes and compliance measures.
- Diversification of Offers: Expanded into affiliate programs with stronger compliance measures.
- Outcomes: Maintained a trustworthy brand image, adapted seamlessly to regulatory changes, and sustained revenue growth.

Case Study 6: Micro-Influencer Affiliate Success

Overview: Explore how a micro-influencer maximized affiliate revenue within a niche community.

Strategies:

- Community Engagement: Actively engaged with a niche audience through forums, groups, and social media.

- Micro-Influencer Partnerships: Collaborated with other micro-influencers for joint promotions.
- User-Generated Content: Encouraged and featured user-generated content in promotions.
- Outcomes: High engagement rates, increased trust within the community, and elevated affiliate conversion rates.

Case Study 7: Leveraging Seasonal Trends

Overview: Learn how an affiliate marketer capitalized on seasonal trends for sustained success.

Strategies:

- Seasonal Content Calendar: Developed a content calendar aligned with peak seasons and holidays.
- Limited-Time Promotions: Created urgency through limited-time offers and exclusive promotions.
- Email Campaigns: Utilized targeted email campaigns to alert subscribers about seasonal deals.
- Outcomes: Consistent revenue spikes during peak seasons, increased subscriber engagement, and a predictable annual revenue cycle.

Each case study in this chapter offers a unique perspective on the diverse ways affiliate marketers have approached challenges, seized opportunities, and achieved success. By studying these real-world examples, you can glean valuable insights to inform your own strategies, adapt to industry changes, and drive your affiliate marketing efforts towards sustainable growth.

9.1 Success Stories in Affiliate Marketing

Affiliate marketing has been a transformative force for individuals and businesses, providing opportunities for financial success and entrepreneurial growth. Here, we showcase inspiring success stories from the world of affiliate marketing, illustrating the diverse paths to achievement within this dynamic industry.

1. Pat Flynn - The Passive Income Guru:

Background: Pat Flynn, the founder of Smart Passive Income, started his affiliate marketing journey by sharing his experiences in building passive income streams.

Key Strategies:

- Transparency: Pat openly shared his successes and failures, building trust with his audience.
- Value-Driven Content: He provided valuable content, including detailed case studies and actionable tips.
- Diversification: Beyond affiliate marketing, Pat explored other income streams, creating a well-rounded business model.
- Outcome: Pat Flynn's success story showcases how transparency, value-driven content, and diversification can lead to sustained success in affiliate marketing.

2. Michelle Schroeder-Gardner - Making Sense of Cents:

Background: Michelle started her blog, Making Sense of Cents, to share her journey towards financial freedom.

Key Strategies:

- Consistent Blogging: Michelle consistently produced high-quality content on personal finance and lifestyle.
- Course Creation: She diversified her income by creating a successful affiliate marketing course.
- Email Marketing: Michelle built and nurtured a strong email list, leveraging it for affiliate promotions.
- Outcome: Michelle's story exemplifies how a combination of content consistency, product creation, and effective email marketing can lead to substantial affiliate income.

3. Rae Hoffman - The Affiliate Marketing Veteran:

Background: Rae Hoffman, an industry veteran, has been a prominent figure in affiliate marketing for over two decades.

Key Strategies:

- Early Adoption: Rae recognized the potential of affiliate marketing early and positioned herself as an authority.

- Networking: She actively engaged in industry events and built a strong network of connections.
- Adaptability: Rae adapted to industry changes, staying relevant through evolving trends.
- Outcome: Rae's success story highlights the importance of early adoption, networking, and adaptability in achieving longevity in affiliate marketing.

4. John Chow - From Blogger to Affiliate Mogul:

Background: John Chow, a prolific blogger, turned his attention to affiliate marketing to monetize his blog.

Key Strategies:

- High-Ticket Affiliate Products: John focused on promoting high-ticket affiliate products in the online marketing niche.
- Branding: He built a personal brand through his blog and social media presence.
- Automation: John automated aspects of his marketing funnel for efficiency.
- Outcome: John Chow's journey underscores the potential of combining high-ticket affiliate products, branding, and automation for substantial affiliate earnings.

5. Kirsty McCubbin - The Authority in Tech Affiliates:

Background: Kirsty McCubbin, known for her tech-focused affiliate marketing, built her authority in the competitive tech niche.

Key Strategies:

- Niche Specialization: Kirsty honed in on the tech niche, becoming a go-to resource for tech-related product reviews.
- Video Content: She leveraged video content on platforms like YouTube for product reviews and tutorials.
- Affiliate Transparency: Kirsty openly disclosed her affiliate relationships, fostering trust with her audience.
- Outcome: Kirsty's success story emphasizes the power of niche specialization, video content, and affiliate transparency in building a thriving affiliate business.

6. Jason Stone - The Millionaire Mentor:

Background: Jason Stone, aka Millionaire Mentor, achieved success through a combination of affiliate marketing and social media.

Key Strategies:

- Instagram Presence: Jason built a massive following on Instagram, showcasing his lifestyle.

- Affiliate Partnerships: He collaborated with brands and promoted products through his Instagram platform.
- Consistent Branding: Jason maintained a consistent brand image across his content.
- Outcome: Jason Stone's story demonstrates how combining a strong social media presence with strategic affiliate partnerships can lead to substantial income.

7. Grace Lever - The Online Business Maven:

Background: Grace Lever, an online business strategist, utilized affiliate marketing as part of her broader business model.

Key Strategies:

- Strategic Partnerships: Grace formed strategic partnerships with businesses aligned with her brand.
- Affiliate Training: She created courses and resources to educate others on effective affiliate marketing strategies.
- Community Building: Grace fostered a supportive community around her brand.
- Outcome: Grace Lever's success showcases the potential of strategic partnerships, education, and community building in the affiliate marketing space.

These success stories demonstrate that there's no one-size-fits-all approach to affiliate marketing. Whether through transparency, niche specialization, social media dominance, or strategic partnerships, each story provides valuable insights into the diverse paths that lead to success in the dynamic world of affiliate marketing.

9.2 Learning from Failures

Failure is an inevitable part of any journey, and in the realm of affiliate marketing, setbacks can often serve as powerful teachers. By examining mistakes and learning from failures, affiliate marketers can adapt their strategies, refine their approaches, and ultimately pave the way for future success. Here are key lessons to glean from common failures in affiliate marketing:

1. Lack of Audience Understanding:

Failure: Failing to truly understand your target audience can result in promoting irrelevant products or services.

Lesson: Take the time to conduct thorough audience research. Understand their needs, preferences, pain points, and aspirations. Tailor your content and promotions to resonate with your audience's specific interests.

2. Overemphasis on Short-Term Gains:

Failure: Prioritizing quick wins over long-term value can lead to promoting low-quality products for immediate gains.

Lesson: Focus on building trust with your audience. Prioritize high-quality products and services that genuinely benefit your audience, even if it means slower initial returns. Long-term trust translates to sustained success.

3. Ignoring Regulatory Compliance:

Failure: Neglecting to stay informed about and adhere to relevant regulations can result in legal issues and damage your reputation.

Lesson: Stay abreast of legal requirements and guidelines related to affiliate marketing in your industry and region. Ensure that your promotional strategies align with these regulations to maintain credibility.

4. Relying Solely on Paid Advertising:

Failure: Depending entirely on paid advertising without diversifying traffic sources can lead to vulnerability during changes in algorithms or ad policies.

Lesson: Diversify your traffic sources, incorporating organic methods such as SEO, social media, and email marketing. A balanced approach reduces reliance on a single channel and enhances overall resilience.

5. Neglecting Mobile Optimization:

Failure: Overlooking the importance of mobile optimization can result in a significant loss of potential conversions from mobile users.

Lesson: Ensure that your website, landing pages, and promotional materials are optimized for mobile devices. A seamless mobile experience is crucial in capturing and retaining a broader audience.

6. Inadequate Tracking and Analytics:

Failure: Insufficient tracking and analytics can lead to a lack of insights into the performance of your campaigns.

Lesson: Implement robust tracking tools to monitor key performance indicators (KPIs). Analyze data regularly to identify what's working and what needs improvement. Informed decisions based on data lead to more effective strategies.

7. Lack of Transparency with the Audience:

Failure: Failing to disclose affiliate relationships can erode trust with your audience.

Lesson: Be transparent about your affiliate partnerships. Clearly disclose when you stand to gain from a promotion. Honest and transparent communication fosters trust, enhancing the likelihood of audience engagement and loyalty.

8. Poorly Designed Landing Pages:

Failure: Sending traffic to poorly designed or confusing landing pages can result in high bounce rates and low conversions.

Lesson: Invest in creating visually appealing and user-friendly landing pages. Clearly communicate the value proposition, and ensure a seamless journey from click to conversion.

9. Neglecting Relationship Building with Merchants:

Failure: Failing to establish strong relationships with affiliate program managers and merchants can limit opportunities for collaboration and special promotions.

Lesson: Actively engage with affiliate program managers. Communicate your goals, seek additional resources, and explore collaborative opportunities. Building strong relationships opens doors to exclusive offers and valuable insights.

10. Inflexibility and Failure to Adapt:

Failure: Resisting change or failing to adapt to evolving industry trends can result in stagnation.

Lesson: Stay informed about industry developments, emerging technologies, and changes in consumer behavior. Be adaptable and willing to pivot your strategies to align with evolving market dynamics.

11. Unrealistic Expectations:

Failure: Setting unrealistic expectations for immediate success can lead to frustration and premature abandonment of strategies.

Lesson: Recognize that affiliate marketing success often requires time and persistence. Set realistic goals, track progress, and celebrate incremental achievements. A patient and measured approach contributes to long-term success.

12. Failure to Test and Iterate:

Failure: Neglecting to test and iterate on strategies can result in missed opportunities for optimization.

Lesson: Implement A/B testing for various elements, including headlines, calls-to-action, and promotional strategies. Use data-driven insights to continuously refine your approach and enhance performance.

In affiliate marketing, failures are not endpoints but rather stepping stones toward improvement. Embrace each setback as an opportunity to learn, adapt, and refine your strategies. By incorporating these lessons into your affiliate marketing journey, you'll be better equipped to navigate challenges, build a sustainable business, and ultimately achieve lasting success.

Chapter 10: Future Trends in Affiliate Marketing

The landscape of affiliate marketing is dynamic, shaped by evolving technologies, consumer behaviors, and industry innovations. As we look ahead, several trends are poised to redefine the future of affiliate marketing. Understanding and embracing these trends will empower marketers to stay ahead of the curve and unlock new opportunities for success.

1.   Influencer Collaboration Reinvented:

Trend: The evolution of influencer marketing will see a more sophisticated approach to collaboration, with influencers becoming strategic partners rather than mere affiliates.

Why: Brands will seek long-term relationships with influencers, fostering authenticity and deeper connections with their audiences. Influencers will have a more integral role in product development and storytelling.

2.   Rise of AI and Machine Learning:

Trend: The integration of artificial intelligence (AI) and machine learning (ML) will revolutionize affiliate marketing strategies.

Why: AI-driven algorithms will enhance targeting precision, optimize content delivery, and personalize user experiences. Marketers will leverage machine learning for predictive analytics, allowing for more informed decision-making.

3. Advanced Attribution Models:

Trend: Attribution models will become more sophisticated, moving beyond last-click attribution to offer a holistic view of the customer journey.

Why: Marketers will adopt multi-touch attribution models that consider various touchpoints, providing insights into the entire conversion path. This approach will lead to a more accurate assessment of the contribution of each marketing channel.

4. Voice Search Optimization for Affiliates:

Trend: With the increasing prevalence of voice-activated devices, affiliates will focus on optimizing content for voice search.

Why: Voice search optimization will become crucial as consumers adopt voice-activated assistants. Affiliates will adapt content strategies to align with natural language queries and conversational search patterns.

5. Blockchain for Transparent Transactions:

Trend: Blockchain technology will be harnessed to enhance transparency and security in affiliate marketing transactions.

Why: Smart contracts on blockchain will streamline payment processes, reduce fraud, and ensure fair compensation for affiliates. Transparency and traceability will be paramount in building trust among all stakeholders.

6.   Niche-Specific Affiliate Platforms:

Trend: The emergence of niche-specific affiliate platforms will provide tailored solutions for marketers operating in specialized industries.

Why: Marketers in specific niches will benefit from platforms that understand the unique dynamics of their industry. These platforms will offer specialized tools, analytics, and affiliate programs catered to niche audiences.

7.   Sustainable and Ethical Marketing:

Trend: Ethical and sustainable marketing practices will become integral to affiliate strategies as consumers prioritize socially responsible brands.

Why: Affiliates will align with brands that demonstrate a commitment to environmental and social responsibility. Sustainable practices in packaging, sourcing, and production will influence consumer choices.

8.   Video Content Dominance:

Trend: Video content will continue to dominate affiliate marketing strategies, expanding beyond traditional platforms.

Why: Short-form and long-form video content will be utilized across social media, streaming services, and emerging platforms. Video will remain a powerful tool for engaging audiences and showcasing product features.

9.   Cross-Device Tracking Solutions:

Trend: Enhanced cross-device tracking solutions will address the challenge of tracking user behavior across multiple devices seamlessly.

Why: As consumers switch between devices, marketers will adopt advanced tracking technologies to maintain a cohesive understanding of user journeys. This will enable more accurate attribution and personalized targeting.

10. Augmented Reality (AR) Integration:

Trend: Affiliates will explore opportunities for integrating augmented reality into their marketing strategies.

Why: AR applications will allow consumers to virtually experience products before making a purchase decision. Affiliates in industries such as fashion, beauty, and home decor will leverage AR for immersive promotional campaigns.

11. Personalized and Dynamic Content:

Trend: The demand for personalized content experiences will drive the use of dynamic content creation and delivery.

Why: Marketers will leverage data to dynamically adjust content based on user preferences, behaviors, and demographics. Personalized content will enhance user engagement and increase conversion rates.

12. Subscription-Based Affiliate Models:

Trend: Subscription-based affiliate models will gain prominence, offering recurring revenue streams for marketers.

Why: Marketers will explore partnerships with subscription-based services, earning ongoing commissions for each subscription renewal. This model aligns with the growing popularity of subscription-based business models.

13. Integration of Social Commerce:

Trend: Social commerce will become an integral part of affiliate marketing strategies, blurring the lines between social media and e-commerce.

Why: Marketers will leverage social media platforms with built-in shopping features, allowing users to discover and purchase products seamlessly. Social commerce will provide new avenues for affiliate promotions.

14. Interactive Content for Engagement:

Trend: The incorporation of interactive content, such as quizzes, polls, and interactive videos, will rise in affiliate marketing campaigns.

Why: Interactive content enhances user engagement, encouraging active participation. Marketers will experiment with gamified experiences and interactive elements to captivate audiences.

15. Compliance with Privacy Regulations:

Trend: Stricter privacy regulations will necessitate a heightened focus on data protection and compliance.

Why: Marketers will prioritize user privacy, implementing measures to secure user data and ensure compliance with global privacy regulations. Transparent communication regarding data usage will be crucial in building trust with consumers.

By staying attuned to these emerging trends, affiliate marketers can position themselves for success in a rapidly evolving landscape. Embracing innovation, adapting to changing consumer behaviors, and leveraging cutting-edge technologies will be instrumental in navigating the future of affiliate marketing.

10.1 Emerging Technologies and Opportunities

As the digital landscape continues to evolve, affiliate marketers are presented with exciting opportunities fueled by emerging technologies. Understanding and harnessing these innovations can propel affiliate marketing strategies to new heights. Here are key emerging technologies and the opportunities they bring to the affiliate marketing space:

1. Artificial Intelligence (AI) and Machine Learning (ML):

Technology: AI and ML algorithms enable data-driven decision-making, predictive analytics, and enhanced personalization.

Opportunities:

- Dynamic Targeting: AI-driven algorithms optimize targeting by analyzing user behavior and preferences.
- Predictive Analytics: ML models forecast trends, aiding in proactive strategy adjustments.
- Personalized Recommendations: AI enhances the personalization of product recommendations, improving user experience.

2. Augmented Reality (AR) and Virtual Reality (VR):

Technology: AR and VR technologies create immersive and interactive experiences.

Opportunities:

- Virtual Product Try-Ons: Affiliates can utilize AR for virtual product demonstrations, allowing users to "try before they buy."
- Interactive Product Showcases: VR experiences can transport users into virtual showrooms, enhancing engagement with affiliate promotions.
- Enhanced Content Experiences: AR elements in print or digital content create interactive and engaging experiences for users.

3. Blockchain Technology:

Technology: Blockchain ensures transparent, secure, and decentralized transactions.

Opportunities:

- Transparent Transactions: Smart contracts on blockchain enhance transparency in affiliate marketing transactions.
- Fraud Prevention: Blockchain minimizes fraud risks by providing an immutable and traceable record of transactions.
- Fair Compensation: Smart contracts automate affiliate payouts, ensuring fair and timely compensation.

4. Voice Search Optimization:

Technology: Voice-activated devices and natural language processing technologies drive voice search.

Opportunities:

- Optimizing for Voice Queries: Affiliates can optimize content for conversational and voice-based search queries.
- Featured Snippets and Position Zero: Capturing position zero in search results becomes crucial for voice search visibility.

- Voice-Activated Promotions: Integrating voice-activated calls-to-action in content for seamless user interaction.

5. 5G Technology:

Technology: The widespread adoption of 5G networks promises faster internet speeds and lower latency.

Opportunities:

- Rich Media Content: Affiliates can deliver high-quality, interactive content with reduced load times.
- Real-Time Engagement: Live streaming, virtual events, and real-time interactions become more accessible.
- Enhanced Mobile Experiences: Faster connectivity enables seamless mobile experiences, crucial for mobile affiliate strategies.

6. Chatbots and Conversational Marketing:

Technology: AI-powered chatbots facilitate real-time interactions and personalized communication.

Opportunities:

- 24/7 Customer Support: Chatbots provide continuous support, enhancing user experience.

- Lead Generation: Chatbots engage users in conversation, aiding in lead generation and qualification.
- Automated Affiliate Assistance: Chatbots can assist users in finding relevant affiliate products and offers.

7. Progressive Web Apps (PWAs):

Technology: PWAs offer app-like experiences through web browsers, providing offline capabilities.

Opportunities:

- Enhanced User Experience: PWAs offer faster load times and seamless navigation, improving user experience.
- Offline Access: Users can engage with affiliate content and promotions even in offline mode.
- Push Notifications: Affiliates can send push notifications for timely promotions and updates.

8. Internet of Things (IoT):

Technology: IoT connects devices, enabling data exchange and automation.

Opportunities:

- Smart Affiliate Products: Affiliates can promote IoT-enabled products, tapping into the smart home and wearables market.
- Data-Driven Insights: IoT data can provide valuable insights into user behaviors and preferences.
- Cross-Device Marketing: Integration with IoT devices allows for personalized cross-device marketing.

9. 3D and Interactive Content:

Technology: 3D modeling and interactive content technologies enhance visual and interactive experiences.

Opportunities:

- Immersive Product Showcases: Affiliates can use 3D models for immersive product showcases.
- Interactive Tutorials: Interactive content aids in providing engaging tutorials and product demonstrations.
- Enhanced Storytelling: 3D and interactive elements elevate storytelling in affiliate content.

10. Edge Computing:

Technology: Edge computing brings processing closer to the data source, reducing latency.

Opportunities:

- Faster Content Delivery: Affiliates can deliver content with lower latency, improving user experience.
- Real-Time Personalization: Edge computing enables real-time processing for personalized content delivery.
- Improved Security: Processing data at the edge enhances security by reducing the exposure of sensitive information.

11. Personalization Engines:

Technology: Personalization engines leverage AI to tailor content based on individual preferences.

Opportunities:

- Hyper-Personalization: Affiliates can create highly personalized content journeys for users.
- Behavioral Targeting: Personalization engines analyze user behavior to deliver relevant affiliate promotions.
- Predictive Personalization: AI predicts user preferences, anticipating their needs for tailored recommendations.

12. Quantum Computing:

Technology: Quantum computing processes complex computations at unprecedented speeds.

Opportunities:

- Advanced Analytics: Quantum computing enables more complex and rapid data analysis.
- Optimized Algorithms: Affiliates can leverage quantum algorithms for more efficient optimization strategies.
- Cryptographic Security: Quantum-resistant cryptography enhances the security of affiliate transactions.

These emerging technologies open doors to innovative strategies and redefine the possibilities within affiliate marketing. Affiliates who embrace these opportunities will not only stay ahead of the curve but also create immersive and personalized experiences that resonate with the evolving expectations of digital consumers.

10.2 Staying Ahead in a Dynamic Landscape

In the ever-evolving landscape of affiliate marketing, staying ahead requires a proactive approach, adaptability, and a keen eye on emerging trends. Here are essential strategies to navigate the dynamic affiliate marketing landscape and position yourself for sustained success:

1. **Continuous Learning and Industry Awareness:**

- Stay Informed: Regularly update your knowledge on industry trends, technological advancements, and changes in consumer behavior.
- Attend Conferences: Participate in affiliate marketing conferences, webinars, and workshops to gain insights and network with industry professionals.
- Follow Thought Leaders: Keep an eye on thought leaders, industry blogs, and reputable publications to stay abreast of the latest developments.

2. Embrace Emerging Technologies:

- Adopt Innovations: Embrace emerging technologies such as AI, blockchain, and immersive experiences to enhance your affiliate strategies.
- Experiment with New Platforms: Explore new advertising platforms, social media features, and emerging channels to reach diverse audiences.
- Leverage Automation: Use automation tools to streamline repetitive tasks, optimize campaigns, and free up time for strategic planning.

3. Data-Driven Decision Making:

- Utilize Analytics: Leverage analytics tools to gather actionable insights into user behavior, campaign performance, and market trends.
- A/B Testing: Implement A/B testing for various elements in your campaigns to optimize for the most effective strategies.

- Predictive Analytics: Explore predictive analytics to anticipate trends, understand consumer preferences, and make informed decisions.

4. Build a Strong Online Presence:

- Optimize Your Website: Ensure your website or blog is well-optimized for user experience, speed, and mobile responsiveness.
- Social Media Engagement: Actively engage with your audience on social media platforms, fostering a community around your niche.
- Content Quality:* Create high-quality, valuable content that resonates with your audience and establishes your authority in your niche.

5. Diversify Traffic Sources:

- Explore New Channels: Diversify your traffic sources by exploring new advertising channels, social media platforms, and content distribution networks.
- Invest in SEO: Implement sound SEO strategies to enhance organic traffic, improve search engine rankings, and increase visibility.
- Email Marketing:* Build and nurture an email list for direct communication with your audience, promoting products, and sharing valuable content.

6. Establish Strong Relationships:

- Affiliate Networks: Cultivate strong relationships with affiliate networks and program managers to access exclusive offers and stay informed about industry changes.
- Collaborate with Influencers: Explore collaborations with influencers in your niche to expand your reach and tap into their engaged audience.
- Connect with Peers: Join affiliate marketing communities, forums, and social groups to exchange insights, share experiences, and stay connected with industry peers.

7. Prioritize User Experience:

- Mobile Optimization: Ensure your affiliate promotions, website, and content are optimized for mobile devices to cater to the growing mobile user base.
- Page Load Speed: Improve page load speed to reduce bounce rates and enhance user experience.
- User-Friendly Design: Create a user-friendly design with clear navigation, compelling visuals, and intuitive layouts.

8. Agile Adaptation to Trends:

- Monitor Consumer Behavior: Stay attuned to shifts in consumer behavior, preferences, and emerging market trends.

- Adapt to Platform Changes: Be agile in adapting to changes in algorithms, policies, and features on advertising platforms and social media.
- Experiment with Content Formats: Explore different content formats, from video to interactive content, to align with changing consumer engagement preferences.

9. Compliance and Ethical Practices:

- Stay Compliant: Keep abreast of privacy regulations, advertising standards, and legal requirements relevant to affiliate marketing.
- Ethical Promotions: Prioritize ethical and transparent promotional practices to build trust with your audience.
- Disclose Affiliate Relationships: Clearly disclose your affiliate relationships to maintain transparency and credibility with your audience.

10. Strategic Scaling and Diversification:

- Scale Wisely: Scale your affiliate business strategically, considering factors such as audience growth, profitability, and market saturation.
- Diversify Income Streams: Explore opportunities for diversifying income streams, such as creating and selling digital products or offering consulting services.
- Global Expansion: Consider expanding your affiliate marketing efforts to new geographic markets, adapting strategies to diverse cultural preferences.

11. Network and Collaborate:

- Join Affiliate Networks: Join reputable affiliate networks to access a wide range of products, services, and promotional opportunities.
- Collaborate with Brands: Build partnerships with brands directly for exclusive promotions, co-branded content, and tailored opportunities.
- Engage in Cross-Promotions: Collaborate with other affiliates or influencers for cross-promotions, expanding your reach to new audiences.

12. Customer Feedback and Iteration:

- Seek Feedback: Actively seek feedback from your audience through surveys, comments, and social interactions.
- Iterate Based on Insights: Use customer feedback to iterate on your strategies, improve user experience, and tailor promotions to audience preferences.
- Adapt to Feedback: Be open to constructive feedback and adapt your approach based on insights gained from audience interactions.

By incorporating these strategies into your affiliate marketing approach, you'll not only navigate the dynamic landscape effectively but also position yourself as a forward-thinking and adaptable marketer. Staying ahead requires a combination of industry knowledge, technological savvy, and a commitment to delivering value to your audience in innovative ways.

Conclusion

In the culmination of "Affiliate Marketing Mastery: Harness the Power of Affiliate Marketing to Build a Lucrative Online Business in the Digital Age," we've embarked on a journey through the dynamic realms of digital entrepreneurship. As the digital age unfolds, affiliate marketing emerges not just as a strategy but as a mastery—an art form that, when wielded with insight and innovation, has the potential to sculpt lucrative online empires.

Embracing the Evolution:

Our exploration began with an understanding of the digital age, recognizing the seismic shifts in consumer behavior, technological landscapes, and the evolving nature of online business. In this age of constant transformation, staying ahead necessitates a mindset attuned to change, an openness to innovation, and an unwavering commitment to learning.

Foundations of Affiliate Marketing:

Delving into the fundamentals, we dissected the very core of affiliate marketing. From deciphering the mechanics of affiliate programs to understanding the symbiotic relationships between affiliates and merchants, a solid foundation was laid. It became clear that success in this realm rests on the mastery of nuances—the ability to discern profitable niches, select high-converting products, and navigate the intricate web of affiliate networks.

Crafting Compelling Content:

Central to our journey was the creation of compelling content—a narrative that captivates, educates, and influences. From content marketing essentials to the intricacies of SEO strategies, we unraveled the art of crafting digital experiences that resonate with audiences in an ever-expanding online universe.

Establishing Your Presence:

The landscape of affiliate marketing extends beyond content creation. Building a robust online presence through websites, blogs, and social media platforms became a pivotal chapter. In this digital arena, where first impressions are digital handshakes, the significance of a well-designed website and strategic social media engagement cannot be overstated.

Maximizing Affiliate Revenue:

Our exploration of affiliate marketing mastery culminated in strategies to maximize revenue. From effective promotion techniques to the alchemy of optimizing conversion rates, every tactic was designed to elevate the affiliate marketer from mere participation to true mastery—a conductor orchestrating a symphony of revenue streams.

Overcoming Challenges and Scaling:

As the journey unfolded, we confronted challenges head-on. Saturation, competition, and industry changes were not roadblocks but stepping stones. Through insights on adaptation, resilience, and the art of scaling, the path to sustained success was illuminated. The affiliate marketer emerged not as a passive participant but as a dynamic force shaping the industry.

Into the Future:

Our odyssey concludes by gazing into the future, where emerging technologies beckon and opportunities abound. Influencers redefine collaboration, AI, and machine learning usher in a new era of precision, and immersive experiences through AR and VR become the norm. Affiliate marketing mastery is not static; it evolves with the pulse of innovation, and those who embrace these emerging trends are poised for unparalleled success.

The Power of Your Mastery:

In the closing pages of this journey, remember that the power of your mastery lies not just in tactics but in the fusion of knowledge, creativity, and adaptability. Your journey as an affiliate marketer is a testament to resilience, continuous learning, and the unwavering belief in the potential of the digital age.

So, as you step into the affiliate marketing arena armed with insights, strategies, and a mastery honed through the digital age, remember that your journey is not just about building an online business—it's about crafting a legacy, harnessing the power of affiliate marketing, and mastering the art of digital entrepreneurship. May your endeavors be as boundless as the digital realm itself, and may your mastery shine brightly in the ever-evolving landscape of online success.

www.ingramcontent.com/pod-product-compliance
Lightning Source LLC
Chambersburg PA
CBHW080532060326
40690CB00022B/5105